*EXECUTIVE Guide to*
Business Success through Human-Centred Systems

**Springer**
*Berlin*
*Heidelberg*
*New York*
*Barcelona*
*Budapest*
*Hong Kong*
*London*
*Milan*
*Paris*
*Tokyo*

Andrew Ainger, Rukesh Kaura and Richard Ennals

*EXECUTIVE*
*Guide to*

# Business Success through Human-Centred Systems

 Springer

Andrew Ainger
Information Engineering Group
Human Centred Systems Ltd
Beaumont
Burfield Road
Old Windsor
Berkshire
SL4 2JP, UK

Richard Ennals
Professor of Business Information Technology
Kingston Business School
Kingston University
Kingston-upon-Thames
KT2 7LB, UK

ISBN 3-540-19929-2 Springer-Verlag Berlin Heidelberg New York

British Library Cataloguing in Publication Data
Ainger, Andrew
    Executive Guide to Business Success Through Human-Centred Systems. – (Executive
    Guides)
    I. Title  II.  Series
    658.3124
    ISBN 3–540–19929–2

Library of Congress Cataloging-in-Publication Data
A catalog record for this book is available.

Typeset by Richard Powell Editorial and Production Services, Basingstoke, Hants RG22 4TX
Printed by Athenæum Press Ltd, Gateshead, England
34/3830-543210   (Printed on acid-free paper)

# Contents

# Preface

This book is about people and skilled work. There has been much turmoil in the business environment about how to best manage the balance between people and technology, at a time when pressures for cost reduction are ever greater.

Our argument is that people are central to business success, and the appropriate use of technology should support their needs. This is not always easy in practice.

We work in a period when change occurs in ever-shortening cycles. Black-and-white solutions may seem attractive, but the long-term consequences are rarely advantageous. A new system is required, building on lessons from the past.

Human-centred systems build upon core skills of the workforce within a rich, emancipatory environment, utilising the benefits of technology. Change can be embraced to achieve competitive advantage and mutual benefit.

The three authors are, respectively, engineering director of an innovative international manufacturing company; analyst for an international merchant bank; and university business school professor. The book is intended to offer a new synthesis of theory and practical experience, derived from recent British and European collaborative programmes.

We are grateful to our colleagues and families for their tolerance during the writing of this book. Even human-centred books impose pressures on busy people.

*Old Windsor, Brighton and Kingston, June 1995*  A.A.
R.K.
R.E.

# Introduction

## Why Read this Book?

Management has lost touch with the job to be managed. General managers are expected to have an eye for the bottom line, and to develop a professional, detached view of the processes for which they are responsible. Such a perspective makes it easier for them to justify downsizing, letting their subordinates go, and prepares them for their own enforced departure.

Recession has demanded a rationale for redundancy. As financial pressures have limited the scope to meet the aspirations of the workforce for investment, training and improvements in pay and conditions, managers have sometimes welcomed an official position to use in their defence.

Although the prevailing economic climate provides ample evidence to justify pessimism, and the continued ratcheting down of companies and of government expectations, it remains true that optimism is more fun. The human-centred systems approach to management, organisation, people and technology is based on confidence in people and in their capacity to interact in economic activities for mutual benefit. One way out of recession, and into sustainable growth, is to believe in people and in their capacity to work together. With the appropriate technology, which is becoming available on a commodity basis, like cornflakes they are sold under different brand labels. Competitive advantage can be achieved by appreciating the potential of the human resource.

The human resource has been under-appreciated, in both the manufacturing and the service sectors. Partly this has been a problem of confidence. All too often, managers have come from a social background different from that of the managed, and have been reluctant to take the risk of trusting the workforce. Overcoming this reluctance is the new entrepreneurial challenge.

During the 1980s financial engineering came to dominate, at the expense both of engineering R&D and of industrial relations. That bubble has now burst, and success now depends on managers and workers, who find themselves in a new, collaborative relationship, after many layers of hierarchy have been stripped away. This book presents a framework to support such collaboration, drawing on long-established traditions of working life research (e.g. Göranzon and Josefson 1988) and practical case studies, some presented in its appendices. This framework involves a radical reinterpretation of a number of modern concepts of management, and offers a new synthesis.

# What is the Role of Technology in Human-Centred Systems?

Recent decades have seen pioneering research efforts devoted to exploring the role of technology in co-operative working, culminating in major projects where commercial organisations have demonstrated their commitment to alternative approaches. A notable example, fundamental to this book, is the work on human-centred computer integrated manufacturing systems, based on insights from Mike Cooley (Cooley 1977, 1988, 1990) and Howard Rosenbrock (Rosenbrock 1990, 1992). Commercial and financial support came from BICC, their subsidary Human Centred Systems Ltd, Rolls-Royce and many other European commercial organisations, with matching funding from the European Commission ESPRIT and DELTA programmes. In the UK the Department of Trade and Industry has taken the work forward with the MOPS Programme (Manufacturing, Organisations, People and Systems), in which the BESTMAN project is seen as a continuation of the European-funded work.

In terms of technology, work in human-centred systems is no longer exceptional. The average buyer of a personal computer has come to expect as standard a windowing environment with a graphical user interface driven by a mouse, possibly with some speech input facilities. Most organisations have come to assume that their personal computers should be networked, enabling colleagues to communicate and share information horizontally, rather than just reporting vertically as in the past. Standard commercial package software supports groupworking.

The technology is there: the problem is to know how to use it to human advantage, particularly in an organisational context. Managers may be poorly equipped to deal with this, having spent a decade or more focusing on the model of individual competition and competitive advantage. They are ill-prepared to exploit the potential for collaboration and information sharing. Human-centred systems enable us to take a fresh look at the business of management, taking account of people using technology in an organisational context.

# What will you learn?

Recently there has been a vogue for management texts that purport to reduce the complexity of management tasks and problems to simple formulae; however, guarantees of success all too often turn out to be subject to the particular circumstances in which the author in question has worked. In reality, managing organisations is largely a matter of managing people, and people cannot sensibly be reduced to formulae. Instead, this book celebrates the richness of experience and knowledge that people bring to organisations, and seeks to provide a broader set of cultural contexts in which to come to terms with enduring complexity and uncertainty.

Automated systems, or sets of official procedures, should be seen as nothing more than ideologies given a more respectable name. Real-time automatic systems require us to suspend human judgement in favour of preprogrammed solutions, despite the enduring uncertainty of the environment in which the systems operate. Such procedures are designed to reduce dissent and enhance bureaucratic authority. It will often be more than the average individual's job is worth to challenge the authority and application of official procedures, particularly when accompanied with the imprimatur of a British or international standards body.

Human-centred systems enable their users, or more properly their members, to transcend such limitations. In human-centred systems, technology is there to support and extend human judgement, not to replace it. Human decisions need support because it is assumed that there is no one "best way", but that any decision will need to be supported by the team of people involved. The presentation of management in terms of human-centred systems authenticates the experience of those who have seen advanced technology support basic mistakes, or have seen rigid management disregard the experience and insights of the workforce for mutual disadvantage.

This book offers hope, and it invites participation. There is no best way to manage complexity: we need to share experience and insights.

# The Role of Case Studies

We are not offering instant solutions. The approach of longitudinal case studies enables us to follow chosen example situations over time, reflecting on particular problems and dilemmas that are raised. Case studies do not tend to provide recipes for easy success for the casual reader. They may instead induce a feeling of humility, as the message is brought home about the complexity of real-world situations, and the problems of change over time. What remains constant is the human-centred set of values of the principal protagonists.

In this book, frequent reference is made to a number of long-term case studies, such as in Volvo and the BICC/Human Centred Systems Ltd projects. These are dealt with at length in the five appendices, and many readers may wish to turn to one of these to whet their appetite at the outset.

Fundamental to our approach is an appreciation of the importance of reflecting on experience, of learning from mistakes. This requires the capacity to accept criticism, and to divulge information that is not always comfortable or convenient. The public relations adviser would prefer us to concentrate on success, suppressing discussion of failure. The marketing specialist wants simple messages, and does not want to be troubled with technical details. We argue that it is no longer honest and reputable to talk of management and business while disregarding technical details.

# Human-Centred Systems as a Critique

The logic of business is to abstract from the human level to organisational and market imperatives. It becomes all too easy to declare people redundant, and call in management consultants. The human-centred systems movement has drawn on ideas and experience from across Europe, bringing together diverse traditions from cultures which pre-date the industrial revolution. As business expands, it draws in those from related academic areas such as psychology, sociology, social administration, education and computer science. Those who are aware of the complexity of their home disciplines will not take kindly to simplistic conclusions, and may welcome a context in which debate is still considered legitimate.

With the collapse of communism and the more widespread adoption of the market approach to the economy, it becomes all the more important to draw on the cultural insights of professionals in the different economies and societies concerned. Businesses cannot be reduced to simple financial calculations; they depend on human understanding, which transcends the following of simple rules.

# Knowledge-Based Industry and World Markets

Successful businesses are based on people making effective use of technology. Knowledge, the contemporary tool of production, has altered the way business is run. It has made change an everyday occurrence, and there is a need for a new approach to business. The old rules no longer apply, and the separation of hand

and brain has taken on a new meaning: the clarity has been blurred with new technologies and working practices.

World markets are today more international and dynamic. Customers expect more variety, and increasingly demand more options. This leaves industry with a challenge to reduce lead times, reduce inventories and improve customer service levels, all against a background of highly variable demand patterns.

How can these seemingly conflicting goals be met? What is the appropriate management response? The traditional mechanistic techniques that have dominated manufacturing industry for decades are now in decline, being replaced by a more balanced approach. This approach increases the role of human input, rather than emphasising automation. Technology is developed to fit the organisation. The human-centred approach is a sensible and balanced use of organisation, people and technology.

In the present market economy, all organisations have to be considered as businesses, at least for aspects of their operations. Typically this will imply that financial considerations dominate, and that costs are closely monitored. Profit motivation is of central importance. During the period of industrial capitalism it was seen as appropriate to construct businesses along the lines of industrial machines. People were assigned rules and job descriptions as if they were machines, and the replacement of unreliable humans by technology was regarded as desirable progress.

We have now entered the post-industrial period, when different paradigms are needed. We cannot assume a continuing demand for mass production, but face pressure for customisation and rapid change. This requires flexibility, skill and the exercise of judgement, in a manner that is not consistent with conventional hierarchical organisational structures. New systems are required for sustaining economic growth in the twenty-first century.

In this book we give an account of the theory and practice of human-centred systems, and locate such systems and their application in the broader context of debates on management in a changing industrial and economic environment. There are a number of approaches that have been attracting commercial attention, such as "quality", "groupwork" and "business process re-engineering"; but these are often presented as if they offer formulae for guaranteed success. It is our argument that it is human-centredness that is critical for success in the organisation of the future, and that quality, groupwork and business process re-engineering should be seen as potential means to that end.

The reinterpretation of technology lies at the heart of human-centred systems, providing a new enabling environment, a matrix, in which skill and judgement can be exercised. It is not a device for hierarchical management, but a medium for communication between individuals and groups who take responsibility for their productive activities.

Organisations are undergoing constant change. Current managements derive their power and status from the hierarchical structures of their organisations. The cycle of removal of layers of middle managers is disruptive of operational working, but has left senior managers relatively unscathed. The redundancies are motivated by the search for short-term cost reduction rather than deeper cultural change. Quality programmes tend to concentrate on documenting existing procedures, and then monitoring conformity with the documentation. Groupwork may be little more than a term used to dignify the use of a new generation of network computer software. Business process re-engineering may be seen as a device by consultancy firms to enable them to gain control over key aspects of a business, for example, such as by outsourcing information technology (IT) functions.

It is the human aspects that are critical. At a time when high levels of education and skill are required to meet post-industrial challenges, Britain is introducing a system of vocational qualifications, whose roots derive from the traditional Tayloristic model of scientific management for industrial capitalism. Education and training should themselves be essentially human-centred, yet they are being reduced to factory processes, "delivering" learning.

Human-centred systems derive from roots in European culture, though there is growing enthusiasm for such approaches in Japan. Britain is still torn between attachments to the United States and Europe, and this manifests itself in both politics and the use of technology. Europeans are sceptical of ideologies, and of systems. They have suffered long periods of rule by political dictators such as Hitler and Stalin, driven by inflexible systems of belief. They have seen the collapse of major companies and industries whose systems and structures could not respond to change. They have resisted American claims for the new technology of computers, and have found that methods that replace workers by machines tended to result in an unskilled and unmotivated workforce that is unable to cope when systems failed. European culture has valued individual skill and creativity in a social context, and has rarely respected profit as a goal in itself. Japanese leaders are moving to a similar view.

The collapse of old ways of working in both East and West is currently being experienced as disastrous. We can offer a new paradigm that is grounded in current practice informed by cultural experience. In place of the "unacceptable face of capitalism", and deriving insights from "socialism with a human face", we can point to "business success through human-centred systems".

# Competition in Europe

World markets are becoming ever more international, dynamic and customer-driven. Competition on price alone is no longer a viable business strategy. Customers expect more variety and more options, requiring industry to reduce lead times and to improve customer service levels. This is against a background of highly variable demand patterns. There is pressure to find a simple means by which these goals can be achieved, with a coherent management response. We argue that there is no single best option to suit all, but that several different approaches can be identified. In this book we present the case for the human-centred approach.

Economic opportunities will be derived from the development of new products and the creation of new markets, fully utilising the competence and workforce skills of the organisation. Profit growth will be derived from economies of scope rather than economies of scale. Short-termist solutions may alleviate immediate problems, but they endanger the viability of future growth and regeneration. Time horizons and payback periods need to be re-evaluated. Time is the critical, underrated factor.

Debates on the competitive ability of European companies have focused on their lack of competitiveness when compared with their equivalents in other industrialised countries. The outlook is grim for some of the European partners. Countries like Germany, Denmark and the Netherlands compete well on the world stage, whereas other partners like the UK and France perform only modestly. The 1992 World Competitiveness Report (Institute for Management Development/World Economic Forum 1992) outlines the overall picture; see the excerpt in Figure 1.1.

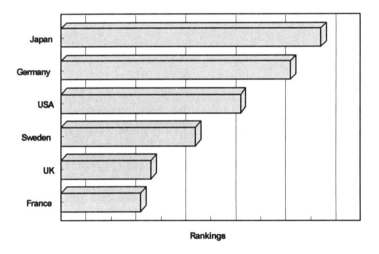

*Figure 1.1    World competitiveness. Source: World Competitiveness Report 1992*

Competitors from Japan have used time as an extremely effective weapon, which has gained them advantages both in product development and in the production and supply processes. There has been a dramatic shortening in product life cycles in many consumer products. For example, Honda has doubled its range of motorcycles in under two years, and Sony continues to launch new versions of its Walkman, several times each month, into its domestic market: the test market is the *real* market.

Japanese industry has comparatively low labour costs, short lead times and effective social organisation of advanced technology. Coupled with this has been an impressive innovation record, which makes life difficult for its competitors.

# Innovation vs. Productivity

Many innovations fail, all companies who do not innovate fail.

*Prince of Wales Award for Innovation Literature, Prince's Trust 1990*

Is there a choice? Traditional technology and operations management impose technical and economic constraints that force many businesses to regard innovation and productivity as a trade-off. More innovation means less productivity, and greater productivity comes from resisting innovation. "Change costs money" is a general attitude, and costs are to be minimised: by "change" is meant change in the product, the process, the organisation and the people. Greater productivity, it is believed, will be achieved by substituting machinery for human labour; costs will be minimised and hence profits maximised.

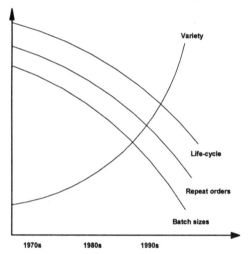

*Figure 1.2  Visible market trends*

Since 1990 we have seen an increasing trend towards the tailoring of products (see Figure 1.2), and the emphasis is on moving from price competition to quality competition. These trends are set to continue into the next century. Key business issues are to reduce lead times, improve customer service and increase responsiveness against a background of highly variable customer demand patterns and changing specifications.

Increased flexibility is vital to meet today's consumer wants. The Seiko Watch Company offers a choice of over 3000 different models. Even more startling is the National Bicycle Company in Japan, who offer 18 different models in a choice of 199 different colour combinations, with six different calligraphies (for their names): a total of 11 231 862 variations!

Competitiveness is a dynamic process, and organisations need to improve continuously. Goals cannot be reached with technology alone; and companies need to recognise that organisation and people are of equal importance. Nor are people and organisation purely "human-factor" issues: strategies need to be established to use organisation, people and technology to meet business challenges. What is required is a balanced approach; many benefits can be achieved without the use of technology.

# Research and Development

The development of new technologies is vital for competitiveness in Europe, but empirical evidence highlights the dominance of the USA and Japan on patent flows. The figures between 1981 and 1988 show a strong net inflow of patents into Europe (see Figure 1.3).

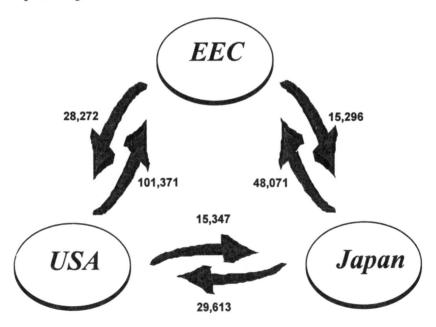

*Figure 1.3    Patent flows in the US/EEC/Japan triad. Source: OECD 1991*

Past years have seen a distinct shift towards a knowledge-based society, and correspondingly a movement towards knowledge-based production. Europe is strong in the fusion of existing technologies into new innovative products, and improvements in technologically intensive innovation. In terms of technology exports and competence, Europe is a world leader (see Figure 1.4). However, in many EC states there is a chasm between the research phase and the commercial application and exploitation of the technologies. The research time horizons that are favourable to industry are not always long-term enough. More collaborative networks of research are required, where traditional divisions are not apparent. For instance, there needs to be more focus on bridging the gap between public and private research, and the role of universities should be re-examined with respect to the development and ownership of intellectual property.

The research dilemma is one that particularly impacts on small- and medium-sized enterprises, SMEs, which have difficulties in keeping pace with innovative developments, and in finding access to R&D activities. This raises problems for European economies, which are predominantly made up of SMEs. More than 90% of all enterprises in the European Community have less than 10 employees, while just over 1% of the organisations employ more than 100 workers.

These problems of SMEs were noted by the manufacturing group BICC, and were a major contributor to its involvement in a series of human-centred systems projects. The first author is the Engineering Manager of Human Centred Systems Ltd, a small company that started as a BICC subsidiary, and is now part of the Information Engineering Group. Its success, detailed in a series of case studies throughout the text and appendices, has been a practical commercial demonstration of the importance of human-centred systems in business.

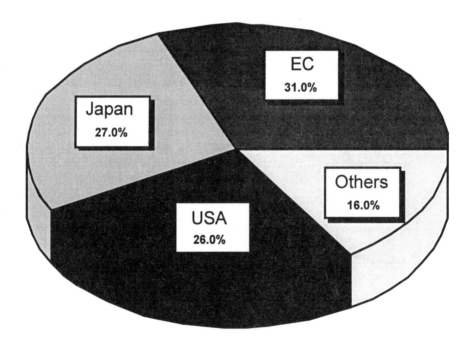

*Figure 1.4    World share of R&D-intensive products. Source: FAST Fine Report, 1993*

Other companies will wish to take advantage of the experience of commercial pioneers, and this book has sought to provide a broader business context. BICC are primarily concerned with manufacturing, but we seek to demonstrate the importance of human-centred systems across the economy, wherever people are working with technology in organisations.

# Insights into Human-Centredness

The future of a modern economy and society depends on the skill and competence of its workforce. Global economies and international competition operate on the back of outstanding technological achievement and advancements. The world grows ever smaller; it is always bright on one side of the planet, creating demand and feedback from others working on the dark side.

This new way of working and organising life requires a new understanding of our surroundings and the tools available to us. The tools should be developed to augment our abilities, yet we have sometimes forgotten this simple fact. Society tends to treat the machine as better than the brain; something is wrong.

Human-centred systems benefit from a rich cultural tradition, and are increasingly being scrutinised with more interest in the light of a failure of present orthodoxies and systems. We can see a transition from a technocentric, or machine-centred, view of work and culture to a more human-centred framework. Lessons have been learned from early pilot work, and experience is being successfully applied.

In this chapter, we give an account of the background of the technocentric, scientifically calibrated view of work (epitomised by Taylor) and provide insights into the foundations and philosophies of human-centred systems.

## Reuniting Hand and Brain

One of Karl Marx's major themes in his early writings (1844) was the division of labour under industrial capitalism, and the resulting alienation of the worker from both the production process and the products of his work. His dream was that following economic, social, technological and political change, the division of labour could be transcended, resulting in a more satisfying and successful work environment. The appropriate use of computers may offer the opportunity to realise part of that dream.

Mike Cooley, an aerospace engineer who has become a philosopher of industry, has studied the separation of hand and brain, concentrating on examples such as Renaissance cathedral architecture, where the separation of the roles of architect and builder became more pronounced (Cooley 1977, 1988, 1990). The complexity of the tasks involved in accomplishing major projects helped encourage the development of separate professions, which have become institutionalised over time.

Cooley's argument has been that this division can now be seen to be both dangerous and unnecessary. It is dangerous for designers to work on products or components without understanding their intended use. It is unnecessary because the new technology of computer-aided design and manufacturing enables designs to be put to practical tests: the same worker can again be designer and builder, making more effective use of skill and tacit knowledge. This has radical implications for work and work organisation.

In this book we pursue this argument, making use of extensive case study experience, with particular emphasis on manufacturing industry. We argue that a similar, and more general, case can be made with regard to information technology strategy for senior executives in companies and organisations of any size. Managers now expect to have computers on their desks as a matter of course, and do not see IT as a wholly separate function where the work is undertaken by people from a contrasting technical background. It is no longer sensible to divide the areas of strategy and operational use of IT, at a time when the technology is omnipresent. IT cannot simply be regarded as an area of expenditure where investments have to be appraised in financial terms. Organisations have become increasingly dependent on IT for their success, and indeed their survival, and are coming to realise that the foundation for that technology is human skill. On this basis, a human-centred approach to IT strategy is essential.

This book takes the argument one stage further, and argues for a human-centred approach to management, reuniting the divided traditions and cultures.

# Taylor and Scientific Management

Frederick Winslow Taylor pioneered the development of scientific management techniques (now termed Taylorism) in the late nineteenth century. Scientific management, as Taylor explained (Taylor 1903), is a process in which "... the workman is told minutely just what he is to do and how he is to do it and any improvement he makes upon the instructions given to him is fatal to success". His technique was aimed at establishing a clear-cut division between mental and manual labour throughout workshops. "It is based upon the precise time-and-motion study of each worker's job in isolation and relegates the entire mental parts of the task in hand to the managerial staff."

Taylor's theories, expounded in his two works, *Shop Management* (Taylor 1903) and *The Principles of Scientific Management* (Taylor 1911), were nurtured and matured during his time at the Midvale Steel Company, which he joined in 1878. In six years, he rose from the position of common labourer to chief engineer. His rise was aided by the firing of a shop clerk for stealing, although Taylor himself states that his advancement was helped because management had more faith in him than other supervisors, as his parents were not from working-class origins.

Taylor's scientific management approach centred on a phenomenon he termed as "soldiering": a situation where the average productivity of a group of workers would equate to the average individual productivity of the least-productive worker within that group. He was convinced that this happened because the compensation system then current did not provide any incentive for workers to commit their maximum efforts.

Taylor proposed and implemented a differential piece-rate system of compensation, which established two distinct rates of pay. Daily quotas were established, and if a worker's output exceeded this daily output rate then all units produced by that individual would be paid at the higher rate. If the quota was not achieved then the lower rate prevailed for all units produced for that day. In order to make the system work, a "fair day's work" had to be defined. Taylor believed that by utilising time-and-motion studies, a one "best way" of performing a job would emerge, and this, combined with the new piece-rate compensation system, would eliminate the phenomenon of soldiering.

His theories, when put into practice, produced impressive and substantial gains in productivity in various organisations:

- At the Midvale Steel Company, where his approaches were first put into practice, productivity increases were realised in each area where his methods were established.
- Taylor was brought in as a private consultant for the Simmond Rolling Machine Company in 1893, where he used his time-and-motion studies to improve methods of operations for inspecting bicycle ball-bearings. The company, which employed 120 women, shortened working day hours and implemented the piece-rate compensation system, as well as firing the least-productive workers. The final outcome of all the changes was that "... thirty-five girls did the work formerly done by one hundred and twenty.... The accuracy of the work at the higher speed was two thirds greater than at the former slow speed" (Taylor 1911).
- In 1898, the Bethlehem Steel Company hired Taylor to improve the processes in its yard gang, where raw materials were unloaded and finished material was loaded onto freight trains. The average productivity was twelve and a half tons per man, with average compensation being $1.15 per day, prior to Taylorism being introduced. Taylor analysed the

processes using time-and-motion studies and established a "fair day's work" as being 47½ tons per man, at a piece rate of $1.85 per day. Productivity and profits were increased with the introduction of the new system.

The next five to ten years saw workers becoming increasingly opposed to the methods of management advocated by Taylor. The movement reached its climax in 1912, when workers in the US steel industry decided to strike. They were fearful of losing their jobs, as had been the case at Midvale and Simmonds in earlier years. Such action was inevitable, as Taylor's methods were inherently incompatible with the ideals of labour unions. Scientific facts were not seen as conducive to collective bargaining. Taylor was summoned by Congress, in order to justify and explain his scientific method of management.

## LOOKING BACK

Taylor's ideas were certainly not as revolutionary as some have argued; the science of shovelling can be traced back to the eighteenth century. As Taylor himself admitted (quoted in Person 1945), "Hardly a single piece of original work was done by me in Scientific Management. Everything that we have has come from a suggestion by someone else" (Taylor 1911). Taylor was not the first to introduce a differential piece-rate system at the Midvale Steel Company. Charles Brinley had already instituted the technique prior to Taylor's arrival. There is also a distinct similarity between the final version of Taylor's work, *The Principles of Scientific Management* and *Industrial Management*, an earlier work about the Taylor system by an associate called Morris Cooke (see Wrege and Greenwood 1991).

Whether the ideas were all Taylor's original thinking or not does not detract from his achievements. He was able to use elements of previous thinking, improving some and adding a new perspective to others, so as to merge new relationships and finally to offer an integrated whole that was revolutionary.

Taylorism was geared towards promoting an individualistic culture of competition between workers. If one worker's piece-rate compensation did not rely on others, there was no incentive to co-operate with others. This created severe problems where work processes required co-operation because of the sequential nature of some of the work. Furthermore, the differential piece-rate system discriminated against the older workers in the organisation, because they were lower in physical stamina than their younger counterparts. Where workers were fired for having low productivity levels, the older ones were at a much higher risk than younger, more physically fit ones. This division of labour demotivated workers, and further discouraged any group work initiatives.

Taylor believed that group interaction was dysfunctional and he discouraged it. He thought it bred wrong attitudes for three reasons (Johansson 1986):

1.   Workers would listen to each other, rather than to supervisors and/or management.
2.   Groups did not allow for individual development or allow for determination of work assignments.
3.   Group determination of what was a fair day's output tended to thwart the scientific determination of optimum production levels.

In fact, Maslow's Hawthorne experiments four decades later (Chapter 5) confirmed that groups tended to determine an "acceptable" level of output.

Taylor was not overly interested in the welfare of workers; he had a narrow outlook, and was unconcerned with the human implications of his beliefs and actions. Taylor viewed humans as "cogs" in the corporate machine, with each job preprogrammed for the worker, leaving no room for individual tacit judgement. Jobs were transformed into tedious periods of activity, requiring a minimum of skills and no incentive to further existing skills, learn new ones or develop personally. Discussing workers loading pig-iron in trucks at the Bethlehem Steel Company, Taylor stated that "... it is possible to train an intelligent gorilla" to do the job of hauling pig-iron.

The underlying assumptions and philosophy behind Taylor's management system had intrinsic weaknesses with respect to management–worker and worker–worker relationships. Had Taylor lived beyond 1915, he might have adapted and evolved his techniques. He advocated the sharing of profits with workers and close relationships between the shop floor and management (although these were far from egalitarian); subsequent advocates of his principles tended to ignore these aspects of his theories.

# McGregor's Theory X and Theory Y

Taylor's view on the human nature of the workers was deeply embedded in McGregor's Theory X. The concept was coined by Douglas McGregor (McGregor 1960), an American academic who was interested in leadership styles, and the associated literature. He asserted that individuals were likely to advocate one of two philosophies about people in organisations.

- Theory X maintained that people avoided work and responsibility, had little or no ambition, and required coercion and direct control. People were therefore punished or rewarded, and their overall activities needed to be directed.
- In contrast, Theory Y maintained that people under the right conditions worked diligently, seeking responsibility and challenge, and displayed commitment and talent. Workers are not resistant to organisational needs naturally, and if they do display tendencies against organisational requirements then it is because of the environment within those organisations.

The ideals and philosophies of W. Edwards Deming, discussed in Chapter 8, lie firmly in the Theory Y notion, opposed to Taylor's views. It has been argued by Tom Gilb that Deming's original approach to quality, as opposed to the way in which quality is now commonly considered, had much in common with the more recent enthusiasm for human-centred systems. Many of the causes we are now arguing for have had supporters in the past: the challenge is to identify the tradition and reclaim the centre stage. New technology may give renewed insights into old problems.

# What are Human-Centred Systems?

Human-centredness is not a concept that can be defined in absolute terms (Brodner 1990; Corbett 1987, Gill 1993). It has developed in different European countries, combining local cultural traditions with a reaction to Taylorism. Human-centred systems are intended to meet demanding and idealistic criteria, in order to deliver improved overall organisational performance.

A human-centred system will not damage the worker's health, nor impair their well-being. It will correspond to the needs of the worker. It will give the worker the opportunity of influencing work decisions, and it will contribute to their personal development. Thus it deals not only with technology, but also with the fundamental principles and practices of organisations.

Human-centred systems seek to accept the present skill of the user, and allow it to develop, rather than incorporating the skill into the machine, and thus de-skilling the human. They allow a greater degree of freedom for users to shape their own working behaviour and objectives. They therefore challenge established divisions of labour. They encourage formal and informal social communications between users, and generally provide a healthy, safe and efficient work environment. This approach sits uncomfortably with rigid hierarchical management structures, but it derives from many pilot projects and has been incorporated into regular practice by companies for sound commercial reasons.

As Europe enters a new era, countries and organisations are looking to human-centred research and development for long-term technological and economic competitiveness. Established paradigms of science are being challenged in the light of new concerns in Europe today, regarding the dangers of limiting the human capability to shape work and technology. Critiques of the Tayloristic approach of attempting to replace human work and skills have drawn attention to human-centred approaches that aim to combine unique human capabilities and skills with the high performance of machines. There is an urgent need for a more balanced approach, one that optimises the combined assets of people, organisation and technology (see Figure 2.1).

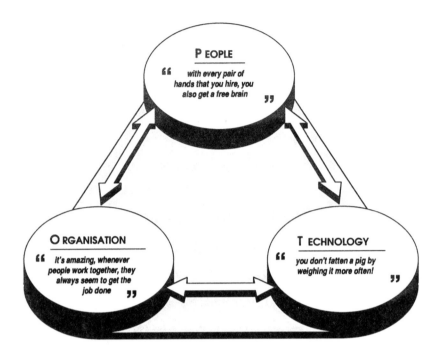

*Figure 2.1     Human-centred systems – a balanced approach. Source: Human Centred Systems Ltd 1993*

This balance and optimisation represents an underlying foundation of human-centred systems. We do not advocate an aversion to technology, but promote the appropriate use of technology and organisation.

Human-centred systems have a long and rich tradition, which in Britain has its origins in movements as an alternative to the Taylorist approach. Advances in microelectronics were beginning to take place, and technology was implemented and utilised without balance. Throughout central Europe, the human-centred approach was gaining momentum, as well as the British tradition of "human-machine symbiosis". In Scandinavia the tradition of "collective resource" was being nurtured and Germany was investing in its "humanisation of technology" initiatives.

Figure 2.2 (*opposite*) outlines some of the major developments that have taken place in human-centred systems design, and also outlines some key research projects underpinning the philosophy.

# Human-Centred IT

In designing and implementing computer systems the goal should be to enhance human skills and abilities, rather than to attempt to replace them. This is the basis of the human-centred process. Tools designed along human-centred lines are intended to enhance the decision-making process of an individual, rather than to provide a "correct" answer. Too often in the past reliance has been placed on the machine to provide black-and-white solutions. However, such solutions cannot be counted upon to form an approximation of the real world, and hence human-centred tools are expected to work with incomplete data, but with the support of human judgement. They provide "degrees of freedom", rather than subjecting the user to demarcations implemented by the designer.

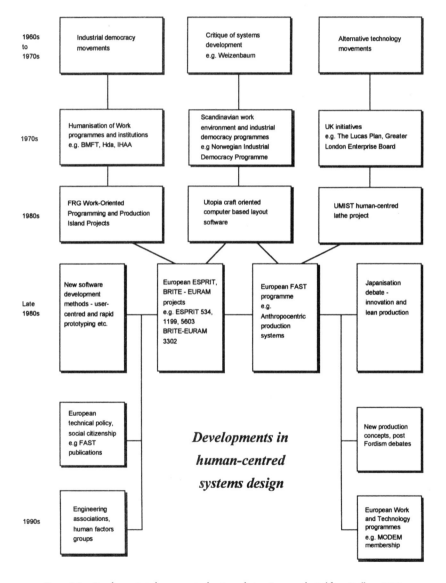

*Figure 2.2    Developments in human-centred systems design. Source: adapted from Badham 1993*

"Human-centred" is a term better applied to processes than to systems. A tool is not human-centred by virtue of possessing a slightly higher degree of user friendliness, or a high level of interaction. Much depends on *how* the tool is used. Just because a tool is designed along human-centred lines, it does not necessarily follow that it will inevitably be used in the same fashion. Conversely, *some* "traditionally" designed tools can be used in a manner consistent with human-centred ideals.

Researchers at the Swedish Institute for Work Life Research (Témpte 1988, 1990) are studying techniques devised by workers in ancient Egypt. The link, they argue, is the need to understand the nature of human skill, and how skills may be enhanced or degraded by the use of different technologies. This is not as abstract as it may first appear. When one looks back into history, the craftsmen of ancient Egypt and Mesopotamia were producing numerous high-quality articles and monolithic structures with very meagre resources by today's standards. One has only to examine the great pyramids of Egypt: the Pyramid of Cheops built around 3000 BC, was constructed with 2 300 000 blocks of stone weighing 5 750 000 tonnes, rising to 150 metres in height. Hard rocks were pounded with dolerite (a resilient stone), in order to detach blocks of stone from a quarry; this was a difficult task for even the master craftsmen, because too hard or too soft a blow would result in a failed block. The only surveying methods available were sightings of the stars, measuring poles and the use of water for levelling. Despite such primitive means, the sides of the pyramid differ in length by only 20 centimetres! (Lilley 1965)

# Designing Tools for Skilled Workers

Increasing numbers of firms and researchers are experimenting with the development of computer programs as useful tools for human experts. Computer-based tools, as opposed to traditional tools, usually allow no direct access to the manufactured object. The user works through an on-screen representation. The consequence is that the man–machine interface has become increasingly important; it is the interface that dictates what a user can do. This limits the use of computer-based tools for complicated or skilled work, where successful operation depends upon the operator's ability, experience and knowledge.

We must stress the integration of computer applications with workers' methods, knowledge and culture at the time of development. Tool-oriented development aims at providing the user with a "toolkit" containing tools that are to be under the control of the user. This tends to present developers with a problem: their knowledge of work processes is limited, and formal specifications do not capture the relevant details from a user perspective.

# Technocentric and Human-Centred Approaches

The design of technocentric systems is dominated by technological considerations; hence users are seen and treated in a mechanistic way. The role of the human is minimised through automation and deskilling; control is transferred to the machine. Technology is viewed as a means of replacing or reducing the role of people.

The human-centred approach, on the other hand, is not in direct opposition to the technocentric approach, but offers a more sensible and balanced use of organisation, people and technology. Many have realised the importance of making use of unique human abilities, and it is easy to overdramatise the human-centred versus technology-centred debate. As Ayres has stated (Ayres 1990):

> *"There is controversy over whether the human-centred approach is more effective than the machine centred approach ascribed to US firms where Taylorism was perhaps more entrenched. This is a false dichotomy, in as much as systems can hardly operate without machines, nor can they function without humans. To achieve low defect rates, it remains necessary to eliminate humans from repetitive jobs where human error can lead to defective parts. On the other hand, human talents are irreplaceable for non-routine functions such as design, planning and general management."*

The way forward lies in a combination of organisational and technological change. The human-centred approach can be the shortest route, as illustrated in Figure 2.3.

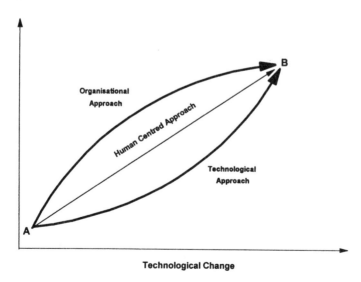

*Figure 2.3 The human-centred approach*

# Introducing New Technology and Methods

The introduction of a new order of things has never been easy, either for the individuals trying to introduce the new order, or for those having to adapt themselves and their lives to it. Management has had a difficult role in changing the thinking of workers, because most of us are resistant to change: as Machiavelli observed, "change has no constituency".

## THE LUDDITES

In England during the early Middle Ages the peasant classes were the dominant proportion of the population, engaged in farming activities. Then structures of society began to change; new attitudes and working practices began to emerge. More and more people came to live in urban communities and to work at crafts in which they shared tools and buildings; merchants marketed the goods that were produced.

As labour-saving devices became more available they were resisted by labourers and artisans. Powered machines were a symbol of perceived injustice. In the fourteenth century legislation restricted the use of mills, and in the fifteenth century came the royal charter granted to the London weavers banning the use of engine looms. Machine-breaking had become a standard practice over time, a response by artisans to merchant abuses. The situation came to a climax during the years from 1811 to 1816, the Luddite period where workers violently clashed with management and the individual warred against the machine (Thomas 1972). Ned Ludd and others led groups of workers who attacked employers operating with unapprenticed workers, paying low piece-rate wages and turning out shoddy products. They destroyed the machines of these employers. It required the intervention of the British army to suppress the guilty groups, who were hunted as violators of the civil peace.

Although the Luddites destroyed machines, this was not their primary purpose, nor mechanisation their main grievance. Their action was a protest against the management and their methods of introducing new forms of working, utilising labour-saving devices and paying low wages. This was during a period of depression, famine and lawlessness. The artisans' income and traditional way of working was threatened and they revolted with fervour. They did not have the modern mechanism of unions or the ability to picket, so they attacked the *symbol* of the movement: the machines.

The spread of machines continued to attract forms of Luddism. Criminal penalties were raised, and the army on occasions called in to protect industrial property. Although rumours were rife, no weapons were discovered in the hands of the Luddites, or in any organised groups.

## DIVISION OR CO-OPERATION

Management have an important role when introducing a new way of working. Workers need to be involved and the need for change needs to be understood; success requires the participation of the workforce. People resent not being involved in the introduction of new technologies, altered values and revised working practices, and begin, overtly or covertly, to rebel against, and to resist, changes that may be necessary for long-term prosperity.

The British tradition has been for managers and workforce to come from different social and educational backgrounds. Industrial-relations tensions have been exacerbated by social class division and mutual suspicion derived from unfamiliarity. The challenge for modern management and modern organisations is to develop a shared co-operative environment, where people are clearly accorded primacy over machines.

## FACTORY OF THE FUTURE: LUDD'S NIGHTMARE

If every tool when summoned, or even of its own accord, could do the work that befits it, just as the creations of Daedalus moved of themselves, or the tripods of Hephaestos went of their own accord to their sacred work, if the weavers' shuttles were to weave of themselves, then there would be no need either of apprentices for the master workers, or of slaves for the lords.

*Aristotle, cited in Badham (1993)*

Physical labour has been viewed with contempt by many in the past. The ancient Greeks saw the activity as a necessary evil fit for slaves and other menials; it was to be avoided at any cost. Time was better spent in search of enlightenment.

Science and technology represent the leading edge in the society that we live in today, as religion was in medieval times. The technological future has crept up on us, and lives and work practices have changed dramatically. Inventions and scientific contributions have renovated our world, and the change has been incremental and sometimes fragmented. The effect of this has been that the future has usually manifested itself in our society before we have the opportunity to say no. Only fifteen years ago we had no personal computers or fax machines, let alone wireless digital communicators capable of interacting with entities around the globe.

Each discernible age has been beguiled by the concept of automation, computerisation and the use of robotics, and as a result industry has been relatively successful in automating and deskilling much of its workforce. Much advanced manufacturing technology has been aimed at implementing the concept of the "factory of the future", complete with lightless buildings manned by gleaming robots feeding flexible systems under computer control. By the end of the 1980s it was becoming evident that use of technology in this manner did not lead to a superior performance, as promised miracles from each generation of technology failed to appear.

# Towards Human-Centred Design

In retrospect, three trends are visible in the history of industrial technology:

1. Artificial means have been substituted for human or animal capabilities. "Horsepower" in an engine was substituted for human energy or animal strength.
2. Knowledge has been mechanically captured in specially designed machines, and ultimately flexibility has increased as "machine intelligence" has substituted for human intelligence and judgement on the plant floor. Automation has deskilled and dehumanised workers in traditional factories.
3. The most recent step has united machine "intelligence" with work done by machines in an attempt to eliminate the human element in operations. The physical resources used in the act of manufacturing are mechanical and artificial.

The technology itself is not to blame. The ideal of automation, that of the self-diagnosing, self-correcting machine that runs without the need for human intervention, has been "fool's gold" for industrial technologists. Too much emphasis has been placed on systems, without serious thought about the necessary organisational and cultural changes that are required concurrently.

Consider a professional soccer player taking a penalty kick: he has full control over which way he can kick the ball, and is not impeded by other players. The objective is to bypass the goalkeeper and put the ball in the net. The player utilises his years of practice and concentration and his "reading" of what the goalkeeper may do, to score. Amateurs may well have missed, and indeed, even the professional may well occasionally miss. The easy part of the problem is seeing the goal, and the goalkeeper. If a machine were to emulate the same task, it would find the problems reversed; "reading" the goal and goalkeeper would be extremely difficult. Actually kicking the ball accurately would be simple; a case of calculating the relevant trajectory and applying the necessary force. In addition, the machine could continually do the same thing, just as accurately, for many, many hours; something that would be quite difficult for the human.

The situation draws attention to what would appear to be quite a simple situation. Humans excel at things that come naturally to us: embodying knowledge, practising judgement, creativity, experiencing emotions and so on. All of these are difficult, if not impossible, for the machine, which excels at precise, repetitive and reliable operations. This could lead to the conclusion that if the strengths of machines are coupled with human skill then many complex tasks can be accomplished. Many engineers have not grasped this, and have reacted to advances in technology by taking a mechanistic view of life in which the human is seen as subordinate to the machine, rather than the other way round. The human is seen as fallible, and the focus is on the weaknesses of the human, rather than on the use of technology to augment and support human strengths.

The complexity and sophistication of modern technology results in designers spending virtually all their creative energies on the technical issues, with little time and thought on the human and organisational issues. Designers' failure to implement technology suitable for the human way of working have led to many disasters. Some illustrative examples include Three Mile Island, Chernobyl, Bhopal and the Swiss chemical spill that poisoned the Rhine. In the US space programme's *Challenger* disaster, NASA personnel made critical decisions without full understanding of the systems; most had made the decision having been awake for 20 hours, with little sleep the night before. Such disasters have been attributed to humans having to work with systems that are outside their "design specifications". There is an alternative approach: we possess the ability to make tools that fit and complement human needs.

## THE VIRTUAL REALITY

Stepping back a few decades, one can recall the time when people walked around the factory, weaving in between machines while they were operating; they could discern what was happening from the sounds, vibrations and even smells of their environment. Skilled workers were able, and encouraged, to detect and solve problems before they occurred, or at least before they escalated to the stage where the machine was out of action for extended periods of time.

Advances in technology have replaced the old-style reading instruments in favour of hi-tech screens, connecting the individual operator to the real world through on-screen representations, graphs and flashing lights, all aglow in dimly lit rooms in order to reduce background "glare". Computers have been isolated from the "action" because of a need for an air-conditioned and controlled environment.

Unfortunately, this has sent people to sleep: no small inconvenience in nuclear power stations. The workers are subjected to a mode of "virtual reality", relegated to watching the meters, waiting for that alarm that signals a failure of the system; this means a job that is 99% monotony and 1% horror and confusion. The irony of the situation is that when things do go wrong, and the human is thrust into the midst of the situation and relied upon to "correct" the problem, there is not necessarily always enough time or information to do so.

## THE STAR WARS FACTORY

The approach taken by many large companies has centred on the realisation of the technocrats' dream; a workplace embedded with high-technology gadgets supporting a highly capital-intensive environment: the Star Wars factory. This ideal was strongly pursued by the General Electric Corporation (GE), who in the early 1980s took the initial steps to realise their dream. The organisation brought together a number of manufacturing operations and built a factory in Charlottesville, North Carolina, to be used as a showpiece for their automation products, in April 1982.

The next three years saw GE experience huge losses, amounting to over $120 million, together with a loss in their market share of CNC (computer-numerically controlled) products. The gross mismanagement of the project had led to a misguided reliance on technology. A company employee, the Engineering Manager Donald Splaun, stated that "management didn't care if there was a need for automation or not .... They just threw the equipment in there and dragged customers to see it." Situations arose, such as robots being utilised to load circuit boards into cabinets, even though a person was still required to hand the boards to the robot! (Burrows 1991)

No corresponding changes were made to the organisation of the company. Little attention was paid to people issues. Indeed, the old fashioned "gun-at-the-head" control approach was put into use. Unions were told that they would have to accept non-negotiable demands or the investment would go to another, non-unionised plant. The investment was primarily seen by GE as a showpiece for their futuristic factory.

Since then, the organisation has modified its unrealistic dreams, and focused on improving quality, employing a balanced and appropriate use of the technology. Automation was made the servant of the production process. In 1991, after numerous organisational changes that centred on people issues, the plant won the Electronic Business Factory Automation Award, and has reversed its losses.

## THE POSSIBILITIES OF INFORMATING

There has been a tradition of recognising that technological advances should be accompanied by a humane approach. The work of Norbert Wiener, including his book *The Human Use of Human Beings* (Wiener 1950), and the work of Joseph Weizenbaum in the 1970s (Weizenbaum 1972), are just two examples.

Shoshana Zuboff, a professor at the Harvard Business School, highlights the possibilities technology possesses for "informating" the users, with information that could never have been gathered in previous times (Zuboff 1988). Robots are capable of capturing data on many variables that could have not been defined without their use. Extrapolating this throughout an organisation yields a continuous dynamic text portraying a picture of how the system is functioning.

In office systems, virtual connections are being established throughout the world; EPOS and imaging systems are capturing vast quantities of data. In this environment, systems are functioning in a much richer context than just automating; they are also informating those with the wit to utilise this resource.

Instead of the "factory of the future" concept, what is required is a system that works in harmony with skilled craftspeople, with technology informating and supporting their work.

## DEMOCRATIC TAYLORISM, OR INDUSTRIAL DEMOCRACY

If the Star Wars factory model is not the profitable or acceptable prescription for running our industries, then what are the alternatives? The manufacturing and services sectors both tend to share the same technocrat's pipedream, whenever consideration is given to the application of new advanced technology and work methods. In both sectors, organisations have been disappointed with results on productivity and competitiveness.

In manufacturing, alternative ways forward have been identified. The first is a manifestation of the Taylor system, but with some important modifications. The system values its workers, allowing for responsibility and training; visions and goals are shared and team-based approaches are encouraged. The system has been transformed from the purely Taylorist application into a contemporary organisation system known as "lean production", which embraces many techniques such as just-in-time production, zero buffer stocks, quality, team-working and so on. Using lean production, the Japanese have been phenomenally successful in gaining huge market shares in the world-wide automotive market, but despite the system's modifications from its Taylorist origins, the underlying production line mentality remains. In fact, Eiji Toyota studied the Fordist paradigm during his visit to the United States in 1950, like his uncle Kilichiro Toyota before him during his visit in 1929, and took the principal concepts back to Toyota in Japan. Shigeo Shingo, one of the inventors of the team production system at Toyota, states that he studied Taylor's *Principles of Scientific Management* and was so impressed that he devoted his life to practising scientific management (Shingo 1989). One and a half million copies of Taylor's *Principles of Scientific Management* have been distributed in translation throughout Japan since its publication in 1911 in the USA.

The second, a holistic alternative to the Stars Wars factory, is epitomised by the efforts of the Swedish car manufacturer Volvo in its Kalmar and Uddevalla plants, where the production line was completely abolished. Work was returned to teams of highly trained and qualified workers (a more comprehensive explanation and insight of the approach can be found in Appendix 1). This approach does not enjoy the same degree of acceptance as the lean-production method, but represents some critical and important issues for consideration when we contemplate the next system to gain competitive advantage.

# The Next Cycle

The late nineteenth century saw the birth of the car industry as a highly skilled craft industry. Demand was low, and each vehicle was built with adapted tools and a great deal of pride. The turn of the century saw the introduction of the Fordist mass-production paradigm, advocated by Henry Ford, who dedicated his life to the production of automobiles; a total of sixteen million Model T Fords were built between 1908 and 1926. Like Taylor before him, Ford was unconcerned with the sociotechnical aspirations of his workers, and he attempted simply to seek an optimum method of production. His thoughts were made clear when he donated $100 million for the building of a school, which he termed as the school of the future (Kraus 1990): "I have manufactured cars long enough ... to the point where I have got the desire to manufacture people. The catchword of the day is standardisation."

The development of lean production by the Japanese in general, but mainly Toyota, is well documented (Womack *et al.* 1990). The system took decades to develop and the quantifiable benefits are impressive. The production paradigm has been viewed by many mainstream proponents as the way forward in factory organisation and human-resource management.

Many surveys and research have been undertaken on the effectiveness of the Japanese system, especially when applied to other countries. Table 2.1 provides one such survey, which compares Japanese transplants in America, providing an insight into the competitive edge that lean production has provided (Rehder 1992).

*Table 2.1   Comparative performances*

|  | Japanese transplants in North America | US plants in North America | European plants in Europe |
|---|---|---|---|
| Productivity | 21.2 | 25.1 | 36.2 |
| Quality (defects/100 veh) | 65.0 | 82.3 | 97.0 |
| Inventories (days) | 1.6 | 2.9 | 2.0 |
| Size of repair area (% of assembly space) | 4.9 | 12.9 | 14.4 |
| Absenteeism | 4.8 | 11.7 | 12.1 |
| Training of new production workers (hours) | 370.0 | 46.4 | 173.3 |
| % of workforce in teams | 71.3 | 17.3 | 0.6 |
| Number of job classifications | 8.7 | 67.1 | 14.8 |

(MIT IMPV World Assembly Plant Survey, 1989)

In contrast, the industrial-democratic approach taken by the Swedes (Volvo, as well as Saab to a lesser extent) has favoured the abolition of the production line. It has not received the wide commercial acceptance enjoyed by lean production. The work at the organisation is viewed as novel but not acceptable in the long term, even though the approach has been in existence within Volvo for over 20 years! Critics of the system have upheld their views with even more zeal since the closure of the pilot plants by Volvo, though the reasons for the closure were complex (see Appendix 1).

It is tempting to state that the next cycle will involve wide acceptance of the lean-production system, as it enjoys commercial success and generates healthy profits. Unfortunately, matters are not that simple. Contrary to popular belief, Japanese approaches are not always notable for worker participation and satisfaction, as has been said when the lean system is implemented in countries outside Japan, and indeed, even within Japan itself. Examples show the confusion:

- Assembly line workers are not accustomed to working intensively, sometimes up to 57 seconds out of 60, often with significant overtime required to achieve production targets.
- The obsession with the elimination of waste is producing high levels of stress; although *kaizen* (continuous improvement) allows individual contribution, the improvement process is restricted by the factory regime, and sometimes by peer-group dynamics.
- The contention that individuals work "smarter, not harder" is in reality workers working "smarter, longer and harder". The Japanese culture is socialised to subordinate individual goals and needs to the collective good. The same attitude is not preponderant in other countries, however, which leads to grievances by the workers and unions.

The working conditions and hours issue is important. How long will it be before we see Europeans or Americans literally "working themselves to death", a symptom that is increasingly prevalent in Japan, known as *karoshi*. A Japanese Automobile Workers' Union (JAWU) report criticises Japan's vehicle industry and highlights the significant overworking of its workforce, which suffers the highest working hours in the world, as well as a low quality of life (see Chapter 8) (Maskery 1992).

Many nevertheless advocate the implementation of the lean system; a landmark MIT study, the International Motor Vehicle Program, provides a compelling case for the adoption of these methods, but not enough attention is paid to the human and political aspects of the system. Table 2.2 provides a summary of the differing perspectives in Japanese transplant companies (Rehder 1992).

Lean production has attracted critics from the unions in various countries. Besides the Japanese Automobile Workers' Union (JAWU) report mentioned above, the Canadian Automobile Workers' Union (CAWU) also criticised the objectives of lean production, which it sees in terms of intensified work, increased management control and the process of undermining unions. IG Metall, the powerful German union, states that lean production is an attempt by management to introduce concepts concentrating on reducing production time and labour costs; benefits to the company should be combined with benefits to the workers, and often they are not.

Table 2.2   *Perspectives of Japanese transplants*

|  | Perspectives of Japanese transplant management, American union, and employee supporters | Perspectives of American dissident union leaders and employees |
|---|---|---|
| Kaizen | Never-ending team quest for perfection for the good of the company and its family of employees. | Personal exploitation, stress, and sacrifice for ever higher production quotas and corporate profits. |
| Stable employment | Employees are company's most important resources. Their loyalty and constant improvements in quality and productivity represent the foundation for their security. | The individual price paid for stable employment is job stress and constant fear of job loss or not meeting punitive attendance policies, demanding work standards, and repetitive work injuries. |
| Develop full human potential | Work smarter, not harder. Continual training fully utilises both mind and body. Recognise full worth, pride, dignity and expertise of all workers. | Work much harder with constant speed-up, appropriate workers, know-how, and improvements to make profits for corporation. Raise standards and reduce any slack in system still further. |
| Multi-skilled self-managing teams | Simplified job classification and work rules, develop high levels of team productivity through multi-skilled team members, autonomy, power sharing and trust. | Self-management and worker control 'an illusion. Reality is high levels of machine-paced management and team peer pressure controls, manipulation and intimidation. Repetitive work causes high numbers of cumulative trauma injuries. |
| Non-adversarial labour relations | Harmony, trust and win-win problem solving among members, union representatives and management to meet common goals of job security, high quality, and productivity necessary to survive in competitive international markets. | Turns traditional union into a company union in which workers get little representation. Culture of co-operation works against team members asserting their rights. Union representatives act as mediators or behave more as if they were training to become managers, which many are. Workers feel intimidated and fear filing a grievance that displeases management. |

# THE AMALGAMATION?

In a market characterised by its need for flexibility, with abilities to change and adapt quickly, the lean-production system is inferior to the Volvo approach. Lean production is a linear mass-production system designed for continuous production runs. The ideology behind the Volvo approach catered specifically for the flexibility required to satisfy consumer demand for tailored specificaions. For example, Volvo's Uddevalla plant completely changed its planning process in late 1992. Dealers around Europe were encouraged to contact the plant directly and delivery of custom-ordered cars was guaranteed within four weeks. Lead times from order to delivery were reduced from 60 to 30 days.

Japan is suffering a labour shortage, and younger members of Japanese society are rejecting assembly-line-related jobs. This is a situation not dissimilar to the one Sweden experienced in earlier years, which led to the implementation of newer working practices. The Japanese young have gone to the extent of coining a phrase for assembly-line workplaces: "3K"; this stands for *kitani* (dirty), *kiken* (dangerous) and *kitsui* (demanding). Japan is facing a similar situation to that which Volvo faced when recruiting staff into their factories.

The way forward lies in a combination of the aspects of different production systems, taking on board the lessons learnt in the Volvo experiences and the Japanese contributions to production management. A synthesis between the Japanese, American and European contributions is required. The trend is already visible:

- Toyota as well as several other Japanese automobile companies have visited Volvo plants on numerous occasions, to learn from the new approaches and perform benchmarking studies. Volvo management maintain that Japanese organisations are the most frequent visitors.
- Volvo now builds cars in the Netherlands in a joint venture with Mitsubishi. The initiative provides the potential for the cross-fertilisation of ideas and experiences between the Japanese and the Swedes.
- Toyota is experimenting with different assembly designs and new work practices at its Tahara and Kyushu plants.
- Honda's NSX sports car, which won many awards, is being built in a factory without an assembly line, by teams of workers. A new approach that denies the moving conveyor system is being nurtured.

It is ironic, and a shame, that at a time when Volvo has closed down its plants that were pioneering the new industrial democracy approach, the Japanese are taking on board the Volvo experiences and evolving them to create a new paradigm to meet the demands of the next century. One can only wonder if Volvo will soon return to emulate the approach that it helped to conceive.

# The New Rules

**3**

## Introduction

Knowledge, the contemporary tool of production, has altered the way business is run. It has made change an everyday occurrence; there is a need for a new approach to business. The old rules no longer exist. The separation of hand and brain has taken on a new meaning; the division has been blurred with new technologies and working practices.

There is more at stake than just intellectual issues; knowledge is also political. We are seeing the gradual breakdown of the current system in favour of an alternative that allows for uncertainty. Human-centred systems do not offer "one best way", but a search for a more rewarding work environment.

In the era of human-centred systems, graduation in a specific field is no longer the passport for an individual's career, but, rather, a portfolio of skills and competences need to be developed and renewed, supporting several career phases. The individual needs to "cross the border" into new spheres of thought and reflection in order to adapt to the new order of things.

We emphasise responsibility and accountability by the organisation to its stakeholders (a wider community than just shareholders). This approach is taking on more mainstream acceptance world-wide in the light of debates on business ethics, the appropriate and imaginative use of technology, and the end of the division of labour.

This chapter explores terms that have been popularised in recent times: teleworking, ethics in business and the new order of things faced by the contemporary worker. Much has been written and debated on these subjects. Each has been presented as a cure for economic malaise. The failure of these techniques has much to do with the rebadging of entrenched past practices, with new labels and symbols. The modern sermons on these themes too often masquerade under pretensions, fashionable words or phrases that hide past patterns of control.

The subjects are not independent, but pieces of an incomplete jigsaw that will perhaps never be completed. Success is derived from effective management of what would seem to be conflicting goals, and from gaining understanding of uncertainty. The themes require a central philosophy to underpin their application in business. It is our argument that human-centredness provides that philosophy.

# Knowledge and the Worker

We must believe the impossible is possible

*Elie Weisel, Winner of the Nobel Peace Prize 1986*

Karl Marx was concerned with progress and civilisation, and did not believe that man, in industrial society, had become truly human, considering him on the contrary, dehumanised. Marx's great hopes for humanity lay in the advent of the communist society. This would bring a new man, entirely different from the alienated worker one found under the evil capitalist system; one who is free, independent and truly human (Marx 1872).

Industries based on knowledge provide new opportunities. In recent times, we have observed start-up companies like Microsoft rise, and become more powerful than established corporations like IBM. In 1992, the market value of Microsoft exceeded that of General Motors for a short period, yet the only indisputable assets that the organisation possessed were the ingenuity and knowledge of its workers.

In today's society, knowledge cannot be controlled and people are becoming increasingly independent. Back in the 1880s, the captains of industry like Rockefeller and Carnegie provided the capital formation to fuel the industrial revolution. The empires that they built owned the means of production, the basis of capitalism, and exploited cheap labour whose providers worked long days in dangerous conditions. The government of that era advocated a *laissez-faire* attitude to the conditions and rights of workers and provided a receptive climate for the grand aims of these empires. The empires effectively controlled and exploited their assets, which included the workers.

Yet did they own their knowledge? Taylor and his disciples did not allow room for workers' knowledge, but bulldozed their judgement into a purified and set pattern of physical working. In a democratic society, no one can *own* someone's brain, nor can they prevent it from moving where it wishes, from institution to institution. This poses a problem for companies, as they can no longer control or attempt to own the contemporary means of production: knowledge. If companies invest in people by means of additional skill and education, then their potential value is increased and thus their potential mobility.

In the USA, 91% of the increase in the number of jobs between 1982 and 1991 has been in the service sector (Reich 1991). A study by McKinsey in 1986 estimated that 70% of all jobs in Europe in the year 2000 would require cerebral skills rather than manual ones. In the 1960s, almost 50% of the workers in the industrialised countries were making or helping to make tangible things, in labour-intensive manufacturing. Estimates suggest that in another thirty years it may be as low as 10%. The figure is already 18% in the USA (Handy 1989).

Those clinging on to Tayloristic work ideas need to reconsider their practices in light of these dramatic changes. We no longer live in a manually orientated environment, but are evolving into a service and information society. The means of production are changing. The old rules no longer exist.

# What is Knowledge?

If knowledge is the new means of production, then organisations need to become proficient in managing it within their corporate systems, in order to improve productivity, competitiveness and working life. Knowledge can be categorised into two components:

- *Codified.* This can be explicit, symbolic or declarative. Codified knowledge is easily discernible because it is factual and concise, and we are all comfortable in its use.
- *Tacit.* This, in contrast, can be implicit, latent or perhaps non-procedural. Tacit knowledge is often ignored because it is difficult to conceptualise and tends to be obscure.

Tacit knowledge is a concept that was coined by Polanyi (Polanyi 1966), who describes it as that which cannot be expressed, but which is known. It is personal knowledge that is gleaned through experience, culture and our interaction with others in society and the workplace. The concept of tacit knowledge needs philosophical underpinnings, if it is not to be regarded as trite.

Tacit knowledge is vital within an organisation, yet it is difficult to articulate and document. It constitutes the missing element in most failures of communication. In outdated, vertically orientated hierarchies, decisions and responsibility are inherently abdicated up the systems, each lacking the tacit knowledge vital for success. The resulting problem becomes ever more difficult and requires additional resources, reducing the chances of a successful outcome.

# The Darwinian Workplace

Organisations, individuals and society are undergoing some of the most radical transformations they have seen for decades, gradually destroying the artificial demarcations that limited the capacity of organisations and their members to behave naturally. Breaking down hierarchies, and hence empowering people to work in a saner and a more creative way, is providing the power for organisations to liberate themselves from nineteenth-century corporate practices. This is leading to a more chaotic (i.e. unpredictable), but increasingly rewarding, workplace.

Such structural changes are having profound effects on employees and employers alike, both of whom are up against the forces of the marketplace, rewarding those who can succeed using the new rules of business, and punishing those who cannot adapt. The darker aspects of downsizing have illuminated the fact that the twenty-first century will not need so many people to perform certain tasks. It is the employees that are taking the longest to come to terms with this fact; the old career ladder does not exist any longer. For instance, since Jack Welch, Chief Executive Officer at General Electric, began the process of streamlining the company's businesses, the number of middle-managerial roles has declined by over 65%. Employees have to become accustomed to increasing responsibility and enriching their current roles.

The Universal Declaration of Human Rights in 1947 guaranteed a choice of job to everyone, but is becoming an anachronism. We see an increasingly large number of ambitious people with huge career expectations competing for an ever decreasing number of jobs that can fulfil their aspirations. Career expectations and associated rewards need to be readdressed in a new light.

The emphasis on devolution of power and increased responsibility has important implications for the individual, who now has to take his career in his own hands. A lifetime of constant learning and education is vital for survival in the newly emerging environment, which demands a flexible worker able to perform in a flexible and adapting environment. Cross-functional responsibilities demand people who are capable of integrating different spheres of knowledge. Learning new skills is important, but perhaps the most urgent challenge is that of unlearning outdated skills and practices.

# Loyalty, the Outdated Concept?

The concept of loyalty in an employee contract is becoming an outdated idea. Corporations are not able to demand employee loyalty, and the worker who works for most of their lifetime with one organisation is becoming a dying breed. A job for life is a contemporary liability. Contrary to popular belief, the majority of the workforce in Japan do not enjoy a job for life; this is a redundant concept in SMEs, whose employees represent in excess of 70% of the total labour force in Japan. On average, the Japanese worker changes company five times within his or her career. Within large organisations, a job for life does exist, but the trend is for workers to be reassigned to SME subsidiaries once they reach a certain age.

Loyalty needs to be earned in a different way; we can observe the emergence of a new psychological contract: increased training and management development in return for commitment and good work. Knowledge has become the means of production, and the organisation is investing in the individual's worth. Organisations need to make a pact with their workers, investing in them and training them in new skills, providing them with the means and tools for managing change. The only certain prospect for the twenty-first century is uncertainty.

## TIME BOMB

Demographic changes have been warning us for some time that emphasis needs to be placed on retraining older workers in our society. The most precious assets any company has are the skill, ingenuity, creativity and imagination of its people. Probably no other single asset is so squandered world-wide. The reasons for this are rooted in our technological development and the organisational forms that surround that technology. In consequence people have come to be viewed as a liability rather than an asset (Cooley 1987).

Our unused resources are important for the success of future economies. The new Darwinian environment is forcing the early retirement of energetic and skilled workers at ages between 50 and 60. The multi-faceted repercussions of the demographic time bomb are going to have radical implications for our social systems. Soon, in the UK, we will see the possibility of one person in five being a pensioner, with pensioners collectively accounting for a fifth of national income.

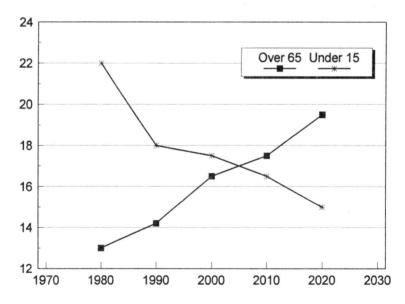

*Figure 3.1    Age groups of total population in the EU countries (percentages). Source: Monod et al. 1991*

All over Europe we are seeing almost a quarter fewer young people leaving school, using 1995 projections compared with 1987 figures; this is resulting in increasing pressure to locate educated individuals for tomorrow's workforce. In the UK, where 43% of youngsters left school in 1986 without an "O" Level in even one subject, the situation today has only improved marginally.

The work of Monod and colleagues (see Figure 3.1, p. 36) (Monod *et al.* 1991) clearly highlights the secular trend in the ageing population within Europe, and supports the statistics indicating a dramatic fall in the young population. In general, estimates suggest that by the year 2000 there will be more workers over 50 than under 30 (European Commission 1993). This fall in the availability of skilled workers is forcing employers to re-examine other sources of skill, such as women who are educated but normally obliged to manage families and homes. Women today comprise nearly half of university entrants.

# A New Form of Work Organisation

Job roles are going to change, and relationships will be redefined. Increasingly, not all employees will necessarily be internal to the organisation, and hence sideways careers will be developed. A striking example of this is the externally managed contracts under which Manpower, the employment services company, provides staff for various large blue-chip companies. There are many alternative models, one of the best known of them being Handy's "shamrock" (Handy 1988) with its three leaves: core professionals, the contractual fringe, and part-time or temporary workers. One can highlight certain characteristics common to this and other relevant models:

- The need for many people to develop sideways careers and a portfolio approach, instead of expecting to climb steadily within a single company and remain with it throughout their working life. This tendency is consistent with the individualistic nature of European work culture.
- The consequential need for each employer to provide each employee with the time, opportunity and resources for continuous professional development. This enables the skills of individuals to remain up to date and marketable.
- The need for all types of flexible working arrangements to be encouraged within each category.

Silicon Valley companies have now for some time provided excellent examples of many elements of the above being put into effect. One may question whether this is an acceptable paradigm; advances in teleworking and the technology to support this type of working would suggest that it is. This acceptance of teleworking further emphasises the need for a portfolio of skills and the advent of, using Handy's terminology, the "shamrock" organisation.

## TELEWORKING

Traditionally, businessmen have operated from home when their trade has not been of a scale that warranted an office, and the individual has had to rely on a basic communications infrastructure. Work patterns were much the same as those that had evolved from the industrial revolution; the norm being a nine-to-five job, usually based in a city centre. The concept of teleworking has only arisen in the past few decades, since the benefits of the practice began to be extolled, especially by IT companies that were well placed to exploit the available technology.

Although teleworking, in effect "working at a distance from your office", covers a whole range of roles in various degrees – offshore workers, mobile workers, and even the executive who takes his or her work home in order not to be disturbed – the term normally has a simple application: the individual working at home with access to a computer and communication facilities (usually phone, modem, fax and so on).

Technology advanced rapidly after the initial enthusiasm, and organisations began to wake up to the potential savings that teleworking could offer. The idea of "hot desking" was born, the term being derived from "hot bunking", i.e. the sharing of bunks by sailors in wartime submarines. Organisations such as IBM and DEC realised that it was not necessary to allocate a desk for every single employee, and that desk spaces and related technology could be shared by different workers visiting the offices on an *ad hoc* basis. Hot desking is like checking into a hotel room, but instead of a room you are allocated a free desk for a set time. As with a hotel room, on leaving you are required to remove all your belongings so that the desk is free for the next user.

The advent of hot desking made the accountants extremely pleased, as cost savings were substantial, given that an office worker requires a minimum of 100 square feet of space (at an annual rental of anything from £10 to £100 per square foot). What accountants did not consider were the human aspects; staff were often plagued by psychological problems stemming from their deep-rooted reliance on personal territory. In today's environment, the emphasis is on cost containment and cost cutting, and human issues are all too often forgotten.

Advances in communication technologies in the 1980s and early 1990s have facilitated a mobile revolution and eliminated traditional technical barriers to widespread use of teleworking:

- An integrated services digital network (ISDN) can support a variety of applications (video, voice) and high-speed data transmissions and is available widely in the UK and most of Europe.
- Electronic mail (email) and telemessaging are allowing remote users to communicate with different domains of workers, easily and without geographical constraints. Workers can work at their own chosen time, within their local time zones.
- Hardware costs have decreased dramatically, and technology has

acquired the status of a basic commodity. Laptop and notebook computers provide a huge amount of power to an individual's lap at low cost, creating a mobile army of workers.

- Mobile communications have become commonplace, with personal digital assistants capable of interacting with corporate systems via wireless communication networks and mobile telephones.
- Answering services are connected to pagers, allowing messages to be stored and retrieved at a later, more convenient time.
- Software has become increasingly intuitive and easier to use, reducing the needs for specialised training requirements. In the UK this has been an added catalyst, because only one in five of the working population uses a computer at work and is hence familiar with the technology; this is low compared with other European countries such as Sweden, where approximately half the population use computers.

The increase in teleworking has much to do with the socioeconomic factors that have supported the trend. The trend was triggered by economic and market factors more than by technological pushes. One of the main features of the last decade has been the huge increase in self-employed workers, a large proportion of whom are highly qualified women.

Experts in the field forecast huge growth rates in the take-up of teleworking. The technology research company OVUM estimates that by the year 2000 the number of teleworkers in Europe and the US will have increased twenty-fold from the 600 000 in 1993 to 12 million (Ovum 1993). In 1993 the Henley Centre for Forecasting calculated that over a sixth of the hours worked in the UK would be worked at home by the mid-1990s; this would represent more than 3.3 million individuals in the UK (Henley Centre 1993). The pace of growth of teleworking has probably been less, but complemented by the development of a "contract culture".

It is not only the technology that is fuelling the trend towards flexible working, and organisations are attracted to the increased flexibility teleworkers can provide. This has been illustrated in the City of London, where recent bombings have highlighted the vulnerability of organisations that are completely located in one place. Teleworking can also have a significant effect on the environment: from the individual's perspective, dispensing with a two-hour commuting journey every day is a huge saving, and teleworking can generally increase the quality of working life; reduced pollution and congestion from less traffic are also wider social advantages.

Several organisations have taken the teleworking route, with the best and earliest proponents being the FI Group (founded as F International), a computer software firm initially employing mainly women programmers working from home, and ICL, whose scheme began in 1969 and in thirteen years had 200 home-based staff. British Telecom has also embraced teleworking as a serious and sustained way of working for a significant number of its staff, and suggests that working at home improves productivity by up to 40%.

Teleworking is becoming an integral aspect of normal work rather than a substitute, but nevertheless a number of important obstacles remain with regard to the human factors. For instance:

- Managers are worried about being able to monitor workers without their traditional methods of direct observation and supervision.
- Personal safety and health is an issue when working at home. Factors such as VDU glare and ergonomically correct seating equipment are not easily controllable or enforceable by the organisation.
- Teleworkers may become lonely and isolated; regular interaction with colleagues boosts morale and helps to keep communication channels open. The psychological problems are numerous, especially for young people who value the social aspects of work. The effects of this can be off-set by having staff based in the office for a proportion of the working week.
- New skills need to be nurtured, most importantly self-discipline, motivation and marketing oneself. Employers may wish to pass responsibility to individuals who are available in the building and "visible" rather than to others who are not.

There are also psychological and associated problems inherent with a lack of simple face-to-face contact. However, there have been advances in technology such as videoconferencing, which promises to become a standard business tool as the technology becomes more affordable. As yet most large corporations disdain to use the facility for big or important deals. The non-verbal nuances prevalent in true face-to-face contact are lost, and as one general manager puts it, "... videoconferencing is fine, but would you play poker over a teleconference link?"

## INFORMATION VILLAGES

The twenty-first century will be marked by its global perspective, as national frontiers mean less and less. Sophisticated information flows and skills will come not only from national marketplaces, but from international information villages. Examples are already prevalent: London Underground approached nine different UK software houses for its new timing system, yet finally settled for a developer in Bombay, at 40% of the cost (*Financial Times* 8 September 1993).

As more people telework, and hot desking increases, the office as we under-stand it is going to change dramatically. A century ago, the first organised offices were beginning to appear, complete with their neatly dressed women typists organised in "pools", surrounded by their "bosses" in offices. A hundred years later, during the 1980s, the tools had changed into VDUs or personal computers, the sexes were a little more equally placed, yet the office has somehow clung to the old, scientific-management mores of a past era.

The past few years have seen the emergence of a new type of workplace. A striking example is the headquarters building for the Scandinavian Airline SAS, in Stockholm, which opened in the late 1980s. Rows of work spaces were abolished in favour of a plethora of open public workspace, meeting areas and atria boasting a variety of artworks. The architect, Neil Torp, has re-engineered the concept of the old workplace, with the new design incorporating shops, restaurants, coffee bars and even a solar-heated "main street" (*Guardian* 3 December 1993). This building, and other examples, highlights the fact that much work is performed outside the desk environment in social situations. The public areas constitute the organisation's "information villages", which nurture a sense of community and teamwork in pleasing surroundings. Such changes are going to have dramatic effects on our psyches, conditioned as they have been to accept the modern-day furniture work organisation, together with its potted plants and filing cabinet imagery, arranged in offices.

## TELEWORKING IN MANUFACTURING

Technology has provided us with the raw materials to build an infrastructure to support teleworking and telenetworking. We can see this phenomenon in effect within the manufacturing sector (see Figure 3.2).

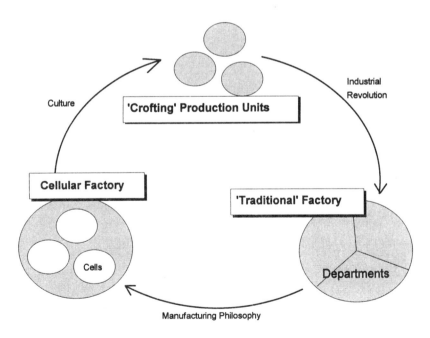

*Figure 3.2 The manufacturing cycle*

Until the industrial revolution, British manufacturing took place mainly in small, "crofting" units. Machining technology brought great advances to industry: the birth of mass production and the beginnings of the end of the traditional crofter. Immense factories were built up, evolving into the "traditional" factory with its separate and distinct departments governed within a strict hierarchy. New philosophies and organisational advances in turn further evolved the situation into the "cellular" factory, which operated on the basis of autonomous business units working in collaboration with other units.

With the changes in organisational cultures and the technology underpinning the infrastructure of organisations today, we are beginning to see a return to crofting production units, and hence the completion of a full circle. The same trend is visible within organisations in other sectors; the flattening of the pyramidal hierarchical system will lead to groups of highly skilled individuals working within formal and informal networks; the idea of a "full-time employee" will not exist as it does today.

# The Ethics of Business

Human values need to be restored to the heart of business, after a period of ethical and technical chaos. Corporate ethics began to grow popular in the late 1970s, originating from a history with its roots in religion and philosophy. The 1980s, characterised by its "greed is good" morality, left in its wake a number of scandals attracting world-wide attention for those involved. Business ethics has become an important issue, but there is a shortage of material to guide management on what "ethics" in business actually involves, and what relevance it has in business decisions. Ethics can still be an afterthought.

We have progressed a long way since the first joint-stock companies such as the East India Company and the Muscovy Company were formed in the sixteenth and seventeenth centuries. These organisations happily dealt in goods ranging from slaves to opium; they were hugely exploitative and profits were their only goal. The industrial revolution followed the same pursuits; cheap child labour working in appalling conditions was accepted as necessary to turn a profit. It was only in the middle of the present century that organisations were forced to wake up to the reality of responsibilities outside the pursuit of profit. Social reforms and the rise of the trade union movement identified the employees as stakeholders of the organisation, together with shareholders. This approach that included a richer moral dimension came to be known as "corporate social responsibility".

Today the theme of business ethics centres on the fact that corporations cannot be run as personal fiefdoms. Contemporary Anglo-Saxon chieftains who believed that they were invincible, like Lord King of British Airways, Lord Hanson of the Hanson Group and the late Robert Maxwell, have yielded, or are beginning to yield. to pressures to become less buccaneering.

Terry Smith's iconoclastic work *Accounting for Growth* (Smith 1993), based on an analysis of City financial practices, has drawn attention to inappropriate boardroom behaviour concerning the use of accounting devices utilised to improve profit figures. Clearly a new boardroom culture is required. That Smith's book cost him his job demonstrates the sensitivity of the issues.

Business ethics continues to receive extensive executive attention, and recent examples in Europe, across the Atlantic and in the Asian Pacific areas clearly illustrate why:

- In the Virgin and British Airways dirty-tricks scandal, British Airways gained access to computer information on Virgin passengers, which was then used in attempts to divert them to British Airways flights. The court cases and commercial ramifications linger on.
- In Italy, Fiat and other large organisations such as Olivetti have issued guidelines for employees in dealing with government officials, political parties and civil servants. Concerns and allegations materialised about wide-scale corruption on public sector contracts. In Fiat, a group executive was arrested in May 1992 for being involved in illicit payments to Government officials in order to obtain contracts. Since then, 12 additional executives have been implicated and investigations have reached senior management, right up to the chief executive. It is not only Italy's largest private company that has involved itself in the politics of the country; the Italian subsidiary of Siemens, the German industrial group, had its managing director arrested following allegations that 10.8 million dollars were paid in order to obtain orders for a city underground railway line (*Financial Times* 5 May 1993), while Olivetti's chief executive officer was jailed for six years as an accessory to the collapse of the Banco Ambrosiano.
- In Spain, investigations into the dealings of the Banco Bilboa Vizcaya (BBV) revealed corrupt transactions with the Spanish Government. In what is known as the Filesa case (after a bogus consultancy company controlled by Socialist Party members), it was revealed that BBV paid almost £1 million to the party, via Filesa, before the 1989 election (*Financial Times* 5 May 1993).
- 1988 saw the prosecution of Michael Milken's firm, Drexel Burnham, for violating US federal securities laws and regulations. The fines ($650 million) were some of the severest in history and contributed to the bankruptcy of the company that followed. In 1991, Salomon Brothers were fined $200 million for violations in connection with its actions concerning Treasury securities.
- The Guinness affair was one of the most prolonged scandals in the capitalist world economies, beginning in 1987 when the chief executive of the beverages company was accused of illegally propping up company shares during the take-over bid for Distillers. Four convictions were the

outcome, with the case finally ending in 1993. The case epitomised the scant regard firms paid to take-over regulations. At the time of writing appeals are pending.

- The case of the Maxwell "missing millions" implicated the late tycoon Robert Maxwell in various abuses, but centred on his looting of various pension funds in his empire, to the tune of £450 million, in order to keep his MCC organisation running. Maxwell died in mysterious circumstances before his dealing became public, and the case implicated a large number of prestigious financial organisations such as Goldman Sachs.

- The Japanese firms Nomura Securities and Nikko Securities have admitted to lending in excess of $250 million dollars to a well-known underworld organisation. 1992 saw the revelation that the company Sagawa Kyubin donated $17 million to prominent Japanese politicians, three of them former prime ministers (Vogel 1992).

- Defence sales are often accompanied by allegations of bribery or attempted bribery to secure contracts. Current allegations involve British companies working in Malaysia, Saudi Arabia and Austria.

The attention to ethics, and established codes, is relatively new in many countries. This is not exclusively the case, and some examples stand out from the crowd. The Swedes have taken the problem of ethical behaviour seriously for some time, establishing an Institute Against Corruption, backed by the Swedish Federation of Industries. Although similar bodies have been recently established in other parts of Europe (e.g. the Institute of Business Ethics in the UK), the Swedish Institute was established in 1923; corruption and bribery are relatively uncommon in Sweden.

## ALTRUISM AND MORALITY

Much business ethics thinking originates from a grounding in moral philosophy and theology, where experts are introduced to the art of management, and then expected to establish frameworks for managers. Not surprisingly, these experts found the precepts of corporate behaviour rather unfavourable, as their thinking and underlying discipline advocates the concept of altruism: an idea that promotes an individual doing good for the sake of righteousness, rather than because that individual will benefit from it. This school of thought has become preoccupied with the evils of the capitalist system. The practical situation is the fulcrum of ethical behaviour debates, and tends to divide those that preach and those that want to practice; abstract theorising makes the adoption of business ethics a difficult and arcane art.

There is a potential contradiction between the ideas of "good, ethical" behaviour and self-interest, and most individuals possess a mixture of altruism and self-interest within a complex personal ethical framework. It is unlikely that individuals have suddenly forgotten the elementary morality learnt while they were growing up. There can be a situation where ethics runs up against the needs of the business; a culture and attitude that was fostered in the 1980s, a decade of greed and nepotism.

A recent European study echoes this sentiment. *Insights into Values in Business*, a study carried out by a Helsinki-based consultancy firm (*Financial Times* 14 July 1993), questioned 70 senior executives in Britain, the Nordic countries and central Europe about the role of business ethics in their organisations. Three in five stated that they carried out their business activities and practices according to a common code of values. Three quarters of these individuals felt that there existed a vacuum between ethical values and actual behaviour. One in five went further, stating that "business necessity overrides such values".

At the heart of the matter is the question of whether individuals are "good" or "bad". Confucianism is divided into two camps: the first represented by Mencius, who stated that man is by nature good, the second represented by Hsuntzu, who said that man is by nature evil. The command-and-control mentality of much of the Anglo-Saxon hemisphere would perhaps consciously, or subconsciously, derive from the latter view. The morality question is difficult, and more thinking needs to be directed towards the optimistic attitude, restoring judgement to the individual.

There is a growing literature on the issue of business ethics and what it actually means. Solomon (Solomon 1992) bases his theories on Aristotle's concept of "virtue", which does not involve radical demands on behaviour, as these are foreign to Aristotle's emphasis on moderation. He advocates that managers are taught to be tough, having to take decisions without consideration of ethical values. He states that this should be tempered with willingness to do what is necessary, with an insistence on doing it humanely.

Others who have the difficult task of implementing ethical frameworks in their organisations also cite from the past. Ian Smedley, a member of the Institute of Directors, returns to the work of Adam Smith: "It is not from the benevolence of the butcher, brewer or baker that we expect our dinner, but from their regard to their own self interest" (Smith 1776). Smedley (*Financial Times* 17 September 1993) argues that profit making should be a priority, and it may be incompatible with the kind of business ethics being currently promoted by academics. Advocates of a free-market philosophy often ignore Adam Smith's earlier work (Smith 1759), which argued for a more stable society where individuals have a moral obligation to their counterparts and community in general.

For concerned managers there is a major challenge. Ciulla (Ciulla 1991) provides some pragmatic clarity in the field. She states that "... the really creative part of business ethics is discovering ways to do what is morally right and socially responsible without ruining your career and company".

## ETHICS IN EUROPE AND AMERICA

Companies on both sides of the Atlantic have begun to incorporate a framework of ethical behaviour in their organisations, but American organisations have acted more widely. In the UK, almost a third of large companies have in place a code of ethics, compared to almost four-fifths of their American counterparts. Business school courses reflect the same picture: the first business ethics course was offered by Harvard Business School in 1915. Estimates suggest that in America alone over 500 courses on the subject are now available, offered by over 90% of the country's business schools (*Economist* 5 June 1993).

In Europe, progress and take-up of business ethics issues has been slower than in the USA, but the approach has been somewhat different. The USA possesses a distinctive legal and social system that has clamped down hard on business misdeeds, spawning a variety of different codes and training programs in the past few years. This proliferation of codes throughout corporate America has much to do with the federal guidelines that were introduced in November 1991, which doubled the median fines for corporates found guilty of crimes such as fraud. The fines would be vastly reduced if the organisation had in practice a suitable business ethics policy. The example below is illustrative (Kahn 1987):

> *"... a fine of $1 million to $2 million could be knocked down to as low as $50 000 for a company with a comprehensive (ethics) program, including a code of conduct, an ombudsman, a hotline and mandatory training programs for executives."*

A real example based on a case study by the US Sentencing Commission is more illuminating (Case 88-266, US Sentencing Commission 1988). A corporation was charged for fraud: overcharging customers for damaging rented cars, and sometimes billing customers for damages they were not responsible for. Prior to the case, $13.7 million were paid back to customers overcharged. The fine given to the corporation was enforced before the new guidelines were put into place; a fine equal to roughly half the pecuniary loss was imposed ($6.85 million). Under the new guidelines, the fines could have varied dramatically in this specific case, as outlined in Table 3.1, with the maximum possible fine being up to $54.8 million (Paine 1994).

*Table 3.1   Fines under federal sentencing guidelines*

|  | Maximum | Minimum |
| --- | --- | --- |
| Ethics program, reporting of crime, co-operation with authorities, and acceptance of responsibility | $ 2 740 000 | $ 685 000 |
| Program only | $10 960 000 | $ 5 480 000 |
| No program, no reporting, no co-operation, no responsibility | $27 400 000 | $13 700 000 |
| No program, no reporting, no co-operation, no responsibility and involvement of high-level personnel | $54 800 000 | $27 400 000 |

The approach taken in the US is to embody a framework of business ethics in formal rules; codes tend to be defined by checklists and guidelines to be used by managers when they are faced with an uncertain situation. This approach is less established in Europe, where ethical traditions can be traced back for hundreds of years. Europe has always taken a rather cynical view of business practices, and Europeans tend not to be so surprised when corporations are accused of foul play. They also resent being lectured on how they should conduct their professional working lives. Business ethics are formulated from a rich and long cultural tradition, which is certainly not universal throughout the world. This presents the managers of global businesses with the thorny issue of attempting to introduce a standardised "list" of ethical behaviours; the subject is not always conducive to this type of formal mechanism.

The contrast between the different legal and ethical environments can have a marked impact on management cultures, by comparison with which technology may be seen as relatively unimportant. Human-centred systems need to operate within a cultural context.

## THE HIPPOCRATIC OATH

An important lesson can be learnt from the doctor's pledge named after the fifth-century BC Greek physician Hippocrates. The Hippocratic oath is a code of professional behaviour, formally taken by those beginning medical practice and the entire process of education in the medical sector, which precedes it, manages to suffuse a strong sense of ethics in future practitioners.

But why should such a code of conduct be applicable only to the medical profession? How about designers who draw up the plans for nuclear weapons of apocalyptic power, and what about architects who design dams that deprive those further down stream of life-giving water and the ability to irrigate their crops? Do we see business and information technology as professions which can set out and enforce codes of conduct? If not, where does that leave the individual practitioner?

## OF ADVANCED TECHNOLOGY

A naive extrapolation of past trends suggests that as computer use penetrates ever more deeply into our lives, computer abuse will follow in line.

*A. Norman,* Computer Insecurity *(Norman 1983)*

Technology in itself is not evil, nor is it able to perform any evils. The latter requires human intervention. Practitioners of advanced technology all too often routinely attempt to transform social, human and political problems into some technical problem, therefore allowing them to solve it rather neatly by technical means. It is a mistake, however, to dismiss technology as merely a tool, and thus not worthy of consideration.

An interesting example is the day, christened "Black Wednesday", on which the UK government spent billions of pounds attempting to prop up a falling sterling rate. The act of opting out of the European Exchange Rate Mechanism (ERM) threw the markets into chaotic turmoil. It is alleged that the activities of that one day cost each British taxpayer £12. The financier George Soros, making full use of expert insights (Soros 1994), combined with available technology to support his challenge to sterling, personally gained in the region of a billion dollars from the *débâcle*. Questions were asked whether such speculation was an undermining of government policies, or perhaps a necessary acceleration of the breaking of unrealistic parities.

The global financial community today is huge business, and we are coming ever closer to the advent of the twenty-four-hour global marketplace. Driving this trend is the advanced technology underpinning this shift, yet it is also perhaps making the markets unstable, as is the use of technology in financial markets! Powerful desktop machines are utilised by every firm operating in one of the world's financial markets, each running advanced software to pick up "trends".

The markets, if they were totally efficient, would display no such trends and stocks would exhibit a "random walk". But the markets are not totally efficient, and advanced technology is being utilised to spot arbitrage opportunities, and to set thresholds where machines, given the authority, will automatically execute deals by selling or buying. In an infrastructure that is increasingly becoming digital, the silicon is being increasingly used to augment, or perhaps even replace, the cerebral carbon. In an environment that is fuelled by rumours, it is not difficult to see machines reacting to, and manipulating the global system, even though they are not physically connected. The link is the market itself. Will we see the day when the system completely tips over? How many more systems, akin to these, are operating in society; who is in control, the human or the computer?

Joseph Weizenbaum, a professor of computer science at MIT, has been concerned with the inappropriate use of technology for some time. He states (Weizenbaum 1987) that

*"... it is virtually certain that every scientific and technical result will, if at all possible, be incorporated in military systems. In these circumstances, scientific and technical workers have a responsibility to enquire about the end uses of their work. They must attempt to know to what ends it will be put. Would they serve these ends directly? Would they personally steer missiles to their targets and watch the people there die?"*

Who is accountable when things go horribly wrong? Is it another case of delegating responsibility up the ladder in this case, until someone is dismissed? Can one human being distance themself from the consequences for others?

# Lessons for Business from the Voluntary Sector

or many in the private sector, management of charities and other voluntary organisations is akin to monastic life. Their own focus has been on profit rather than on people. Although the voluntary sector may be driven by philanthropic motives, increasingly the organisations are facing the same competitive pressures as companies in the private sector, and some are succeeding.

The voluntary sector is big business, yet how big is difficult to determine. There are between 140 000 and 160 000 registered charities in Britain alone, with estimates of 1 in 5 adults involved with voluntary groups in some way; the sector, in spite of its money-box-and-brightly-coloured-stickers image, has a substantial income of 3.5% to 4% of GDP.

In America, the statistics are even more surprising. It is estimated that every other adult works as a volunteer in some capacity, giving an average of nearly five hours per week. This is equal to almost 10 million full-time jobs, which if paid, would represent 5% of GNP (Drucker 1993).

Traditionally, management was the equivalent of a four-letter word in the voluntary sector; it reeked of capitalism, authoritarism and bureaucracy. Voluntary organisations considered themselves above commercialism, and the umbilical link to the bottom line and shareholders. Ironically, commercial pressure and government legislation have now forced the sector to become more management-oriented, and talk of money is paramount. (This is not too surprising, as charities usually do not have an abundance of it.)

What can organisations in the private sector learn from those operating in the voluntary sector? Organisations such as the Girl Guides, which enlists the support of 730 0000 volunteers, caters for 3.5 million members world-wide and yet only employs 6000 paid staff.

## THE MISSION

Look at virtually any American or European company's yearly accounts, and their mission statement will read in terms of financial growth, shareholders' equity and so on; financial numbers are exclusively used to create the next year's mission. Businesses tend to begin any decision by planning financial returns, whereas the voluntary sector begins with the performance of their mission, to which a great deal of consideration and thought is devoted.

The Japanese company statement is rather similar to that of the voluntary organisation, stating what they have to make happen outside the immediate domain, before they can succeed in their own domain.

In the recent statements from the board of Snell & Wilcox, a British electronics firm, we see a commitment to principles of Christian socialism, worker participation and innovative manufacturing. The third author serves as a non-executive director. One objective of the company is to serve as a model for the future.

## THE MANAGEMENT BOARD

The voluntary sector is an anomaly in the world of management, in that it possesses a functioning board and a CEO who is clearly accountable. Charities tend to make effective use of their boards of directors, who are viewed as the major organ of the organisation.

In the private sector, any business failure or media-grabbing event highlights the ignorance of the management board involved; they were always the last to realise that things were going awry. One need only point to the relatively recent Guinness affair, or the British Airways and Virgin "dirty-tricks" scandal, for an illustrative example.

The identification of stakeholders in a voluntary organisation is not clear-cut, as it usually is with private organisations, which are viewed as primarily responsible to shareholders.

## AN ENJOYABLE ENVIRONMENT

Why do individuals give up time to participate in voluntary activities? Not all volunteers are engaged in work that might be termed menial, such as envelope stuffing, or driving the elderly to a week-end break.

Perhaps it is because their jobs do not offer much challenge, not enough sense of achievement and belonging: no mission. Voluntary organisations offer an environment that individuals want to be involved in, most often without financial rewards. Each worker is aware of their contribution to the collective whole, and they have a sense of belonging and participation; they are not just a number. The organisations also have an important social dimension, making a practical contribution and facilitating human networking within the community.

# What Can Be Learnt?

The new workplace has forced much re-engineering of core processes and restructuring of individual roles. Workers and organisations are becoming more accustomed to negotiating voluntary relationships that benefit both sides of the coin. This attitude is fast replacing that of rigid and fixed dependencies, and old-style contracts between parties.

As relationships rely increasingly on voluntary behaviour, much can be learnt from the experiences and the functioning of a voluntary organisation. Corporate values need to be realigned towards the worker as well as the customer; after all, one department downstream in an organisation is a customer of an upstream department, an element of the internal customer chain. Michael Porter (Porter

1990) popularised the value chain of an organisation in strategic terms, but the internal chains that exist within organisations tend to be of a more multi-dimensional nature, inextricably interlinked and interdependent, rather than one-dimensional and systematic.

# Business Process Re-Engineering

Businesses have had a hard time adapting to and understanding the many new techniques for change that they have been offered. In order to sustain a high level of performance in non-homogenous markets, organisations are embracing radical changes in their organisational processes. Enterprises, and indeed whole industries, are developing new systems based on highly ambitious goal criteria, and are shifting their businesses from an activity-oriented strategy to a process-oriented one. The momentum is further enhanced by the fusion and availability of different technologies. This has inevitably required painful pruning, shedding and redefining; the act has caught the imagination, and embodied itself in the term "business process re-engineering" (BPR).

The use of language is important: BPR is necessary to realign processes to post-industrial-revolution business practices and needs, but the language is being used to disguise some elements of the change that is being carried out. Few people understand the language used within the BPR concept (outsourcing, downsizing, etc.), especially by those consultants who would advocate management of key components of business by other entities, including their own. Redundancies are often motivated by cost reduction, rather than by deeper cultural change, creating fear within the organisation. What is required is a robust framework for the future of the organisation, sustaining the process of change.

In this chapter we argue that the human-centred systems framework is one means of providing a paradigm to support continuous process change, and the challenging of traditional entrenched orthodoxies, while providing the means and focus for the regeneration of skills.

# Introduction

The life cycles of many management techniques follow a pattern. The idea is nurtured and blossoms under the influence of business academics and management gurus. The technique promises to be the panacea of that decade. Finally the management consultancies propagate the ideas through the corporate jungle. After a time the myths are challenged, and what remains may be of real value to organisations who are determined to make effective use of the technique.

Arguably, business process re-engineering is in the last stage. According to which management consultants you talk to, the labels "organisational re-engineering", "business engineering", "core process redesign" or one of a number of similar permutations is equally as applicable. BPR promises a revolution and has made a large impact in Europe and the US in the 1990s, which is not surprising because it promises productivity miracles in virtually all industries. An annual survey of senior executives in Europe (by the consultants CSC Index, themselves major players in the BPR consultancy field) found the BPR issue entering the top twenty issues of concern to senior managers at seventeen in 1989. It jumped to number one in 1990 and has been there for three years in a row. BPR's progenitors, Hammer and Champy (Hammer and Champy 1988), define the concept as

*"the fundamental rethinking and radical redesign of business processes to achieve dramatic improvements in critical, contemporary measures of performance, such as cost, quality, service and speed."*

Traditionally, the organisation was viewed vertically, function by function: purchasing, design, manufacturing, and so on. In today's environment this is not applicable, and a more horizontal emphasis is needed. Re-engineering involves transforming the entire organisation by taking a holistic approach, beginning with business units, from the traditional vertical structure to a more horizontal one. The emphasis is on radical change, and transforming an organisation into a horizontal company involves more than just embracing the redesign of core processes. The organisation has to embrace other, related initiatives, to provide an overall structure, such as new reward systems, multi-purpose skills training to strengthen link teams, and a devolution of power into responsibility.

One of the most revolutionary aspects of BPR is that it has the potential to challenge the foundations that twentieth-century organisations have been built on, namely the maxims of Taylorism. This is certainly startling news for the zealots of scientific management, who advocate that work should be broken down into narrow and specialised activities and departments to enable supervision and control. As the wheel turns full circle we see the possibility of the restoration of human values to the industrial process.

## BPR – REAL OR HYPE?

The concept behind BPR is nothing new, but the label itself is relatively recent, having been first used in the MIT research programme "Management in the 1990s", which ran from 1983 to 1987. Arguably, Taylor could be said to have re-engineered industrial production to improve productivity in the early twentieth century and Deming, among others, re-engineered businesses to improve quality (see Chapter 8).

The process of redesigning business processes and operations by cross-functional teams has been an activity that some Western companies have been engaged in for years. Drucker (Drucker 1993) claims that pharmaceutical and chemical companies have utilised similar processes for decades. He traces back re-engineering to the streamlining of retail and ordering stock control that Marks & Spencer pioneered in the 1930s, through the simple use of a cigar box to store vital information from tags torn off by cashiers.

However, although the concept has been around for some years, mass attention has only been relatively recent. The numerous reasons for re-engineering embedding itself as a firm concept in the past few years are as follows:

- The late 1980s and early 1990s saw much of the world experiencing recessionary pressure as well as increasing competitive pressure from global competitors. The emphasis was on becoming a lean and agile organisation, and slashing costs was a primary concern. In the Anglo-Saxon economies, unlike Japan, a further source of pressure came from enthusiastic shareholders, who cheered each successive cutback as a sign of improved performance.
- In the turbulent environment we face, it facilitates survival to focus on key processes and to develop an organisation-wide ability to improve them. BPR promises that the organisation can be redesigned to "do more with less", or at least "much more with the same", which is an attractive proposition.
- Since the mid-1980s, many US and European companies have initiated or accomplished some element of delayering, downsizing and restructuring. BPR is the next logical step in the process.

BPR has far-reaching consequences for the "big corporation" as we used to understand the term, i.e. the type of monolithic corporation now increasingly likened to the dinosaur. Most big corporations have, in recent years, cut their number of layers by 50% or more. Even in Japan, Toyota has streamlined its hierarchy from 20 to 11, while General Motors has reduced its from 28 to 19, and that number is to drop further. Furthermore, within the past ten years, the proportion of the workforce employed by the most prosperous companies from the "Fortune 500" has fallen from 30% to 13% (*Harvard Business Review* 1993). Even more startling, almost 47% of the companies that comprised the Fortune 500 in 1980 did not exist in 1990.

## THE IMPACT ON PEOPLE

Downsizing and delayering should not be confused with process re-engineering, although this often happens: according to Champy (Champy 1993), only 5–10% of companies who claim that they are re-engineering are actually doing so. The term *re-engineering* is misapplied widely, and is usually confused with, or is sometimes a euphemism for, simply laying people off.

That this happens is not surprising, because much doom has been purveyed about the possible repercussions on employment levels. It has been forecast in the *Wall Street Journal*, and in consultants' reports predicted that re-engineering could destroy as many as 25 million US jobs, mainly in service activities. This is unlikely and unrealistic; if this number of jobs were lost, then unemployment rates would be in the region of 25–35%, greater than the rates experienced in the depths of the great depression. Champy's comments (Champy 1993) partially counteract this human-resource impact:

*"Some companies say they've re-engineered when they've done nothing of the sort: they've simply lopped off part of the business.... In many cases, re-engineering creates no net job losses at all, instead its prime objective is to slash cycle time or raise quality. In other instances it can remove between 50 and 75% of the jobs in a particular process, though not in the total organisation."*

This view is consistent with the view taken by many management consultants, whose experience with clients has indicated that the scale of the job loss issue is only relevant if a company goes horizontal from top to bottom, and creates no extra-value jobs, however indirectly. In many cases, companies find that their now improved competitiveness generates considerable extra business, and subsequently work to be done.

The shedding of layers intrinsically affects employee morale. This is clearly illustrated in recent examples, such as IBM's massive misfortunes. Louis Gerstner, the IBM chairman, is having to wield his hatchet in removing "dead wood" throughout the huge organisation that once promised a "job for life". Lord Hanson has been constantly applauded by the City's financial centres in doing the same with his acquisitions from the 1980s, slimming down "surplus" activities in areas such as R&D. One must question, however, if this is the sustainable and human-centred way of running a company over time: academic research has showed consistently that, while fear motivates in the short term, prolonged uncertainty creates a fall in morale, which in turn affects the bottom-line – the very factor needing improvement.

This begs a critical question: who should go? Most organisations have recently encouraged the voluntary redundancy approach, but this is far from ideal, and all too often those who leave are re-employed as contractors at a later date. It is usually the people an organisation can ill afford to lose who end up going.

Organisations benefit from an atmosphere of confidence, rather than fear. Deming, as one of his 14 quality principles (Chapter 8), stressed that promoting fear was bad management and urged executives to "drive out fear" and encourage creativity among junior workers by giving them more responsibility.

Workers cannot perform unless they experience some level of security and are without fear (Deming 1982).

It is not only the junior workers who are insecure; many managers are anxious about the unknown and fear the future. Just as no one ever used to "get fired for buying IBM", no one seems to get fired for calling in the management consultant, brought in to liberate the organisation from its ills. Perhaps it is time to begin the process of believing in the individual, and leaving the changes to the workers themselves; after all, they are the ones who best understand the processes, the business, and, in the end, what needs to done.

These paradoxical situations are difficult to halt, let alone reverse. Organisations need to reflect on their current cultures. Typically many of a company's best people leave and the organisation finds it difficult to attract new blood. This approach is the antithesis of the human-centred process and its view that a company's employees are its greatest asset. When comparing the Anglo-Saxon approach with that of the Japanese, we find our international competitors in the midst of the worst recession for more than twenty years. Their behaviour is in stark contrast to ours, and many large Japanese companies place their emphasis on retaining employees in whom they have invested so much. Most are achieving this by insourcing and pulling work back in from their suppliers.

The consultancy company CSC Index, of which James Champy is chairman, is aware of the human element, the commercial potential of re-engineering and the evident effects on morale. It offers a computer laboratory for modelling the effects on staff morale, with the idea of avoiding trauma by redeployment where available. Such tools, and other temptations offered by the consultants, allow them to feed upon the fears of managers who do not have faith in themselves and their workers.

Considerations of morale make it crucial to have a consolidated re-engineering programme where employees are not subordinate to the process. It is ironic that many organisations introduce a BPR project to remove Tayloristic work axioms, only to fall into the trap of implementing them just as Taylor himself would have prescribed. For an organisation to remove the insecurity of its employees and remotivate them, while retaining the flexibility to adjust its size as necessary, it must involve them in the decision-making process. If people are empowered to feel in partial control of their workplace, then they are better able to accept that change is a way of life.

## A QUESTION OF CULTURE

Change is necessary for sclerotic companies to rid themselves of outdated processes and make the transformation into lean, competitive and creative organisations. Making this radical transformation is a considerable exercise in scope and depth, where the behaviour of many people in the organisation is affected significantly. All the variations of BPR have an effect on the culture of the company; cultural change is not a separate category. The questions are how to manage the change process, and which should come first: the cultural change to help and facilitate the process change, or vice versa?

Drucker's thoughts (Drucker 1993) are clear on the subject, and he is in no doubt that there is little point trying to change an organisation's culture before altering the tasks of the people within it. He provides two reasons:

*"... culture is very largely dictated by the task: take the very distinct cultures of a hospital or a school...culture is very difficult to change – like the drunkard who doesn't hit the bottle again until Monday morning, backsliders always outnumber converts."*

The latter point of this managerial conundrum is painfully obvious to anyone who has initiated or implemented a programme of change. The former is not so clear-cut. The question of cultural transformation is not an easy one, and lessons can be learnt from collaborative initiatives that allow new companies to begin to embrace the process of change. Companies can also benefit from the experience of large organisations that have "really" re-engineered their processes and not just one or two processes in a single subsidiary, and learn from "best practice".

The time scales involved can range from months to years, depending on the culture and business structure of the organisation, before a BPR project is initiated at full steam. Culture is not an abstract concept, but a phenomenon that is constantly evolving and developing. In some cases, notably the situations faced by countries affected by the failure of the communist system in Europe, companies have been thrown into a chaotic environment where a change in culture is being forced through at an incredible rate. Other situations require a gradual change in the mindset and understanding of employees, where a series of initiatives are introduced to communicate new ideas and associated language.

At Bell Atlantic, the Philadelphia-based telecommunication company, a large change programme was initiated in the 1980s. In mid-1992 it took between a fortnight and a month to connect customers to the long-distance carrier of their choice, unless they defected to speedier competitors. By late 1992, waiting time was down to three days, and it was subsequently cut to a matter of hours. To achieve such success, the company had already spent four years on a culture change programme that aimed to replace Tayloristic control mentalities prevalent in middle management. New behaviours, such as empowerment, teamwork and feedback, were encouraged to make the transformation work.

Cigna, the US insurance company, has led a re-engineering programme since the late 1980s and Susan Kozik, its vice-president, has been a leading member of the internal team heading the programme. Experience has taught the company, who have now re-engineered their 10 divisions, not to start a re-engineering programme without first launching a programme of culture change. In earlier efforts, not enough meetings were held to prepare employees for the new language and thinking of re-engineering. Kozik states (Kozik 1992) that

*"... without meetings and other cultural initiatives such as the introduction of team based pay incentives, change tends to be rejected quickly ... it then takes far longer to reap any benefit from re-engineering."*

Bell Atlantic, Cigna and other companies, including those in the BESTMAN consortium, are not isolated in their learning experiences. Successful cultural transformation is arguably one of the most vital ingredients in a successful BPR programme, and cultural changes follow more naturally if employees are working in processes that they themselves have built. The cultural elements have to be right; the financial and emotional costs of changing to a process-oriented business, such as necessary redundancies, are not insignificant. Bringing about a new organisational culture is about people and personalities. This is not conducive to a "right or wrong" checklist, but certain attributes are certainly apparent in successful programmes. First and foremost, the organisation's people should be involved in the decision process, and the BPR concept should be widely communicated throughout the enterprise.

It is the impact of re-engineering on the sociotechnical structures within a company that makes it so difficult to achieve; it entails vast political and human upheaval. Much emphasis is placed on the processes themselves, as well as the systems that act as their enablers. The most significant change is the impact on the organisation's people, their skills, behaviour, values and culture: getting this right is key to successful change.

# Lessons from East Germany

Radical political and economic changes have affected the social stability of Eastern European countries. Companies operating in the former East Germany are facing very significant changes, and subsequently are having to undergo crucial cultural changes in order to survive. They can no longer operate with the same values and behaviours that they nurtured within a state-planned system, and the change to a market economy requires a huge change not only in structures but also in the mindset of employees and employers. The challenges such companies face offer valuable insights into how to change a culture in order to survive, although it is rare for an organisation to have to undergo so radical a transformation in so short a period of time.

One of the more important challenges for managers in the change process is the new concept of strategy: how will actions and products affect the actions of others within the organisation? The previous system focused on units specified in official yearly plans; there was no need for strategy, or the consideration of other parts of the system. Today, within this new strategy, however, different management instruments, many based on the Western world's organisations, are being imported. But it does not necessarily follow, and indeed it is highly unlikely, that this will work; the culture and mindset behind these instruments have not been understood, nor have they been disseminated throughout the company's workforce.

Customers in Germany are no longer hindered by the Wall; East Berlin companies have to compete with West Berlin companies. This puts emphasis on servicing the wants of the official king of the market economy: the customer. This mentality is hugely lacking in former East German companies; in the previous planned economy, companies distributed scarce goods and not all customers had access to them. In the new order of things, overconsumption is rife, and it is suddenly the employees who need to make efforts to make sales occur. Employees are only just beginning to wake up to the idea of the customer.

In the re-engineering of processes in former East Germany, vital cultural changes are not synchronised with organisational changes; this is because the mindsets of individuals are not keeping pace with the structural shifts being imposed. Individuals are having to deal with newly introduced strategies and structures without having the experience and skills necessary to work in them successfully (Antal and Merkens 1993).

Throughout the Eastern bloc, business processes are having to be radically and fundamentally re-engineered in order to survive in the new environment. Their experiences suggest that new structures and processes cannot be effectively sustained, or value added, without the necessary and timely re-engineering of the culture, values and beliefs of the workforce.

All of this suggests that perhaps cultural changes should begin before new processes are put into place; workers should understand the extent of new systems and practices. Economic shock therapy offers no guarantees of success, and exacts a heavy human price.

# Two Degrees of Culture

The end of the cold war thrust defence firms, and others that had relied on government agencies for major elements of the business, into a forced change requiring re-engineering not only of core processes, but also in culture. The need to either convert or diversify organisations in order to create products suitable for civil use requires a profound change in managerial capabilities, realisation of market forces, lessening of bureaucracy, and an encouragement of innovation and entrepreneurial flair.

The fall in defence spending did not happen overnight with the end of the cold war or the destruction of the Berlin Wall. Organisations dependent on military contracts generally suffered a long period of inertia during the 1980s, leading to mass redundancies in the early 1990s. A NEDO study (NEDO 1991) highlighted the need for an effective organisational cultural change in attempts to diversify processes.

Organisations in Britain undertook various routes, like British Aerospace who partially consolidated through the acquisition of Royal Ordnance Factories, and diversified in new business: construction (Ballast Needham), cars (Rover) and property (Arlington). In general, though, there are very few examples of successful change, and as McKinsey reported, US success rates have ranked from low to terrible (Smith and Smith 1992). Indeed, British Aerospace have now reversed their earlier strategy by disposing of non-core businesses.

One of the most famous conversion plans was developed by the shop stewards at Lucas Aerospace in the late 1970s; this was known as the "Lucas Workers' Plan for Socially Useful Production" (Cooley 1987). Despite the commercial validity of the proposals, Lucas chose not to pursue the ideas; the plan and its reception very clearly indicated the politics of change. For instance, workers proposed the manufacture of a heat pump using natural gas, but the proposal was rejected on the grounds of non-profitability. It was later revealed that the organisation possessed reports prepared by consultants indicating the possibilities of a major market for the pump. Lucas failed to support work on conversion, and with the ending of the cold war has faced considerable difficulties. It came too late to the realisation that quality and skill were vital for success in the new culture of the civil market.

The situation faced by organisations dealing in defence products is somewhat similar to the one faced by an organisation undertaking a fundamental re-engineering program: there is a critical need for a unified change in culture. There is also the further question of the valuable resources made redundant, probably people. Experience of attempts in the field of conversion from defence to civil production clearly highlights the problems incurred when there is a reluctance to change.

# Types of Re-engineering

As with most techniques, the extent of applications varies, and BPR is no exception. Henry Johansson and his colleagues (Johansson *et al.* 1993) from the management consultancy Coopers & Lybrand, like others in their field, distinguish between different extents of re-engineering:

- Most common is the type that creates dramatic cost, time and productivity improvements in rather narrow business processes.
- Increasingly popular is the kind that helps a company reach parity in an entire core process, measured through a "best in class" type of comparison, with strategic and effective use of benchmarking activities. This category is typified by an AT&T unit that makes power supplies. Using this extent of BPR technique, the unit has slashed its design-to-delivery cycle tenfold since 1991, from 53 days to 5 days (*Financial Times* 24 May 1993).
- More rare is the occasional process that enables a company to leapfrog way ahead of its rivals by modifying the established and accepted rules of an entire industry. Strategists term this event the achievement of a

strategic breakpoint – when a company's market share moves disproportionately upward as a result of a dramatic improvement in cost, quality, service or lead time. An excellent example of this type of re-engineering is Wal-Mart, which re-engineered its supply chain by replacing its own warehouses and distribution centres with point-of-sale (POS) systems linked to suppliers. The result was an ability to offer customers constantly refilled shelves of branded products at reduced prices.

## Back to the Drawing Board

The essence of re-engineering is "starting over and beginning with a clean sheet of paper". It rejects the assumptions inherent in Adam Smith's industrial paradigm, including the division of labour and hierarchical control. Everything is questioned, and there are no "sacred cows". The BPR technique is a key way of improving business efficiency by examining key processes as opposed to traditional functions and divisions.

Many senior managers are still sceptical, and argue that their business was never engineered in the first place, so how can it possibly be re-engineered? OTR, a Brussels-based consultancy working with BPR, concludes that BPR is based on real principles and that there is genuine value in applying them, but that the current hyperbole is confusing the picture. OTR claims that nobody has re-engineered their whole business, because it is too risky. Even with unlimited funds, organisations do not dare to remove the pillars supporting the business; the business may collapse before reassembly is completed (OTR 1992).

The OTR group advocate measures, elements of which bear more than a passing resemblance to the approach pioneered in the BESTMAN project; leadership from the top, cultural as well as organisational change, and re-engineering a small part of the organisation before expanding to an enterprise-wide transformation. This last recommendation is now being applied to processes of legislative change in areas such as the National Health Service and the Child Support Agency.

## IT the Enabler

Companies are spending millions of pounds on applying information technology to business processes which are donkey's years old and are irrelevant to today's needs.

*John Bennet, Executive Director, ICL*

The MIT research programme "Management in the 1990s", which started in 1983, considered the impact of IT on organisations and managers in the 1990s. BPR was identified as the third of five levels of IT-induced organisational transformation (see Figure 4.1).

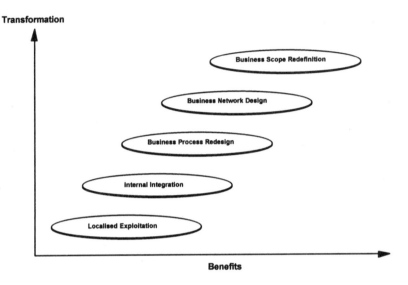

*Figure 4.1    The five levels of IT-induced organisational transformation*

At that time, the latter term possessed a precise definition (though today this sharp clarity has been somewhat obscured): "The use of IT to transform the way in which an organisation works internally rather that simply to automate the way in which it already worked." Organisations have benefited from large improvements in the cost performance of advanced technology, yet office productivity has barely increased in the last decade. Studies (*Financial Times* 10 December 1992) indicate that office workers' output has grown by only 1% during the 1980s, while the amount of time spent in the office has increased by 20%. A report by Policy Publications outlines the research by Morgan Stanley, citing the $800 billion spent on IT in America alone during the 1980s, resulting in an improvement of just 0.7% in service productivity.

In manufacturing, survey after survey has highlighted concerns about the cost of IT and its failure to live up to promises; perhaps this is because technical issues are secondary to the primary and more demanding human issues. One study (Voss 1993) on the success and failure of advanced manufacturing companies in the UK showed that:

- 100% achieved technical success: i.e. they got the systems working.
- 86% achieved increases in productivity.
- 57% realised other benefits.
- Only a mere 14% improved their competitiveness.

The interest in BPR may well respond to the belated realisation by management that vast sums of money were wasted on data processing investment in the 1970s and 1980s. Companies automated old, inefficient functional procedures, instead of first abandoning them, redesigning the rest and then computerising.

In many surveys and reports, such as those by Business Intelligence and CSC Index, research highlights IT as the key to business re-engineering. IT is the enabler that allows the sharing of information and helps to break down barriers and guarded departmental ownership of data; a team-based approach is encouraged. Tools to facilitate group working have gained prominence in organisations that are utilising their existing IT infrastructures and networks to allow workers to interact to a greater degree, regardless of functional or geographical locations (see Chapter 6).

The IT department is no longer a separate entity, and the relationship between the department and the rest of the company is no longer that of a detached process. The emphasis is now on how the process plays a part in the future, and should be regarded as an element of the driving force that helps to shape the BPR programme.

## USING IT AS THE IMPETUS

If IT is the enabler, then the introduction of a new system can be the impetus for changing and updating the outdated process. Unfortunately, this golden opportunity is largely ignored, and IT is used to automate existing processes rather than creating new ones.

IT has the ability to displace completely processes that were based on specialised labour and had all the limitations inherent in paper-based systems. It has the power to capture and process data that can informate, using Zuboff's term, an organisation; such information could never even be collated before. This knowledge can enable individuals to make their own decisions more effectively, and can take on active tasks together with the added responsibility of monitoring.

The tacit assumption, that the worker making the product lacks the inclination or the knowledge to monitor and control the process as well, is steeped in the paradigms emerging from the postwar period. Technology has changed, and processes need to do the same.

Take the interface to the modern computer. The keyboard originated from a design based on mechanical typewriters, designed to slow the typist in order to prevent the jamming of keys. Today, we still cling to this antiquated design, and are still reticent about making the leap to more intuitive interaction processes, like using a mouse pointer augmented by voice command.

Nobody likes to challenge the *status quo*, but those organisations that have the foresight to use IT as the enabling force behind their re-engineering programme will reap huge benefits; the tools are already available, and have been for some time. The remaining challenge is the appropriate and balanced use of the technology to aid individuals in their newly engineered processes.

# Learning from the Factory

Experience has indicated that an appropriate and balanced use of technology in manufacturing (see Appendices 1, 2 and 4) leads to significant productivity gains. BPR allows concepts like "best practice" to be applied to the office environment, just as well as on the factory floor.

Physical layout is important in manufacturing, because moving materials and work in progress around can be costly. Productivity and cost enhancements can be achieved through a sensible organisation of the work without the use of IT: a good example is the German company Klingenberg & Kranzle, who reorganised their factory from a traditional Tayloristic layout to a product-based organisation. The results are shown in Figure 4.2; and other improvements include simplified material flows, easier production planning and improved job satisfaction. These organisational changes led to a 10% increase in direct costs because the role of the shop floor employees was expanded (Kidd 1990).

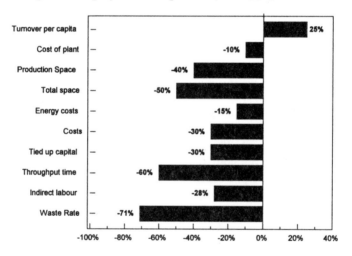

*Figure 4.2   The importance of physical layout*

In the office, delays in dealing with important documents occur because they are passed between too many people, departments and offices, and are subsequently misplaced. As a result, executives spend up to four weeks of their time every year looking for documents, and it costs an average of £75 to find a document that has been misfiled.

Using advanced technology together with BPR, processes can be designed to simplify the workflow by reducing the number of stages involved in a certain procedure. Many productivity improvements have been realised through the use of image-processing techniques and workflow software. Image processing involves the capture of a complete image of a document, after which workflow software automatically forwards the document image on to the relevant worker at the relevant time.

In manufacturing, traditional factories have been re-engineered to operate more autonomously within team-based structures, or cells (further discussed in Chapter 6), with each team responsible for scheduling and production. Members are afforded more responsibility and training in order to gain competence in a wider range of roles.

Recent steps have expanded the re-organisation still further, from a resource-planned organisational structure to one that is operations-managed. Cells have expanded to become autonomous business units, each interacting with other units as and when necessary. Business units embrace all aspects of the process: sales, planning, finance, production and so on.

# Regenerating the Organisation

There is nothing more difficult ... than to take the lead in the introduction of a new order of things.

*(Machiavelli 1514)*

Time and motion shaped the twentieth century: the basis of the scientific management movement, which permeated throughout our society, reorganised not only private and public industry but, in more recent times, municipal government, hospitals and our education sector. It was also a dominant philosophy for President Teddy Roosevelt's Progressives in implementing political and social reforms in the USA at the turn of the century.

In the 1990s, re-engineering has the potential to readdress this orthodoxy, but is it enough? BPR projects do not always deliver improvements in financial performance, and this conclusion has been confirmed by a study performed by the consultants McKinsey & Co. (*Harvard Business Review* 1993). Of 20 companies involved in BPR projects, many cut the cost of their redesigned processes by 15–50%, but only six achieved total cost reductions of above 13% in the business unit concerned, creating at most a marginal rise in earnings.

In many cases, the process was attached to the design of narrow activities within functions. BPR is not a shallow, isolated exercise, and needs to be combined with other elements of change: an educated and trained workforce with new responsibilities; new organisational structures; shared values and skills; and the effective use of (effective) IT.

Managers are becoming increasingly focused and competent at cutting and shedding, but they are not learning how to grow companies. Like the pruning of a rose bush, cutting and shedding are necessary tasks, but if you over-prune then the bush may never recover. Executives are not adding sustained value to an organisation when they restructure a company, and do not stay long enough to help it grow. The recent case of British Aerospace selling Rover Group to BMW, shedding the jewel in its crown, illustrates the point. More recently, British Aerospace has taken the route of outsourcing key aspects of their business, for example their entire IT requirements, which are now controlled by CSC. This shedding and outsourcing of critical elements of their business may have dire consequences on their ability to regenerate themselves; time will tell.

In today's environment, organisations need to focus on better management of their existing assets, through delayering, quality management and re-engineering. To survive in tomorrow's environment, companies need to reinvent their strategies and organisations (Pascale 1992, Hamel 1993).

For the past 92 years, one of the world's greatest innovative companies, 3M, has set itself ambitious targets, including a target of obtaining 25% of its revenues from products that did not exist five years before. It has recently replaced this target with a tougher goal of 30% in the last four years. Furnished with its unique culture, the organisation has continually reinvented itself since its creation, when its founders bought a corundum mine (to use its raw material as an abrasive in sandpaper) which turned out to be "corundumless".

Motorola has risen to the challenge, and has transformed itself into a model of innovation, especially in mobile communications. It has successfully shrugged off what looked like a slide into oblivion, experienced during the 1970s. By re-inventing its strategy, the company is creating the future, through its Iridium project for a global satellite-based cellular communications network. Ironically, the project was the brainchild of a middle manager whose ideas were approved by top management, after being turned down by his immediate superior.

BPR begins the process of shifting the organisation, but like the ideology of continuous improvement, the challenge is to sustain that shift. The need is illustrated by Peters's best-selling book *In Search of Excellence* (Peters 1982), which profiled 43 excellent organisations in 1982, of which 29 are considerably weaker today.

The way ahead for any company is to foresee the next round of competitive advantage and to become the architect of an industry's transformation, like 3M and Hewlett-Packard. This is indeed a tall order for the average firm. To achieve it requires challenging the *status quo* and established orthodoxies, as well as examining the company's underlying paradigm. The human-centred approach begins to provide the necessary framework.

# Empowerment

**5**

## Introduction

Recent years have seen organisations restructuring themselves to meet new challenges. The organisation of the future must be able to achieve more, in shorter time scales and with higher quality levels, and with less people, supported by advanced organisational and technological advancements. Hierarchical control structures are being replaced by flatter processes operating within team-based environments. The consequences are that these new processes require workers to take on more responsibility, and seek additional training and competencies. Empowerment has more dimensions than just the devolution of power, or delegation.

The illusion of control needs to be shattered, and it is the surrendering of this illusion that terrifies many. Taylorism has left such an ingrained mark on management theory that new ways of thinking are seen as unthinkable. Loss of control signifies the loss of a science-based rationality: organisations are seen as unstable and volatile constellations that must be managed. Management in turn becomes an attempt to keep chaotic forces under control.

Many Anglo-Saxon cultures find it difficult to avoid reliance on authoritarian rule, as they have been deeply entrenched in the command-and-control way of thinking. The human-centred ideology welcomes participation, and represents a contemporary approach to democracy. Those who are rejecting totalitarian rule, as in Eastern Europe, are seeking more than just a capitalist import.

Human-centred systems provide the potential for making extensive use of individual capacities in an intelligent and emancipatory way, with workers encouraged to utilise their own ingenuity and judgement. Workers *must* be allowed this autonomy in an organisation run along human-centred lines.

The success of human-centredness depends on shared values and the sense of ownership. We argue that a human-centred systems approach begins to restore accountability and responsibility to the worker, and encourages a longer-term outlook and environment, where mistakes are tolerated and learnt from. This is more than just paying lip-service to the empowerment of individuals.

# Flat Pyramids – the Future?

*"The world of the nineties and beyond will not belong to managers or those who make the numbers dance, as we used to say, or those who are conversant with all the business and jargon we use to sound smart. The world will belong to passionate, driven leaders: people who not only have an enormous amount of energy but who can energise those whom they lead."*

*Jack Welch, Chairman, General Electric (USA)*

Advances in management techniques over the past couple of decades suggest that we are in the midst of the most dramatic transformation in the ways human beings organise themselves since the Chinese invented the pyramidal command structure 2000 years ago. The organisations of the twenty-first century will possess new configurations: networks, lattices, modules and matrices.

Working practices in the next century require a new paradigm, and the flattening of the hierarchical pyramid, increased globalisation, networking and teleworking are all contributing to this fundamental shift. Few management techniques have made such a large impact as empowerment: the key to unlocking the commitment of the workforce.

Empowerment is one of the management concepts that have generated much noise and just as much confusion in the last decade. Planting the concept with managers and shop floor workers usually results in enthusiasm followed by clouds of confusion. Executives and middle managers fear it will undermine their authority, and at worst simply remove their jobs. The more enlightened see it as the only way their business will prosper and survive into the next century.

# Responsibilisation – Is it for You?

The term "empowerment" is used to describe a variety of different levels of involvement, and can itself be misleading, as it has traditionally been used in political circles to signify the gaining of power. Many American pundits prefer the term "high performance", and in France the term empowerment is virtually never used, in favour of what the French call "*responsibilisation*". Ironically the Germans, and German-speaking Swiss, prefer empowerment to their equivalent, "*Ermaechtigung*". Basle-based Ciba-Geigy began using the term "directed autonomy" in their empowerment programme, which management found less threatening.

One of the primary reasons for confusion over the empowerment concept is the old problem of not using pure, common-sense meanings of words. The French term for empowerment, "responsibilisation", is extremely appropriate in this case. Often, the word "empowerment" is used without the balancing concept, responsibility. Peters and Waterman (Peters and Waterman 1988) and Drucker (Drucker 1993) have all continually stressed that empowerment carries with it the need for much greater responsibility.

"All power tends to corrupt, and absolute power corrupts absolutely," wrote Lord Acton. Empowerment, in the contemporary meaning, implies devolving power from the top, further down to lower levels. A balanced organisation today is more horizontal, and placing power lower down may simply corrupt lower down. The emphasis should be on balancing power with responsibility; it is no use retaining power, as many middle and upper managers attempt to, while abdicating responsibilities.

Information needs to be shared, and open communication channels are necessary. Management information systems, and executive information systems, should be reoriented towards employee information systems or enterprise information systems. You can only provide decision-making responsibilities to people who have the information to make intelligent decisions.

## KAREN AND JILL – EMPOWERED BY ASSOCIATION!

The inefficient use of the workforce is a phenomenon that the authors have experienced on several occasions, through involvement with projects partly sponsored by the European Community. The cases of Karen and Jill are illustrative.

ESPRIT project 1199 (1217) is one of the most cited and well-known human-centred research projects in the manufacturing sector. A BICC Technologies unit participated in the UK element of the collaborative project, working together with other UK partners, including a company manufacturing high-specification radio-frequency connectors, whose workforce of 300, mostly female, were responsible for basic assembly-type work which was highly manually intensive. (See the case study in Appendix 2 for more comprehensive details of the project.)

The end of the project saw an open day demonstration at the factory site, based in the south-east of England. Training issues were raised, and it was suggested that, towards the end of the project, two workers should visit the BICC site in order to test, learn and further familiarise themselves with the software that had been developed for the project. The software was created to allow teams, or cells, of workers to conduct their day-to-day work responsibilities with a degree of freedom; it was assumed that the workers would be afforded the autonomy to arrange their own schedules and environment, etc., and hence effective use of the tool depended on the thinking of the individual.

At the time, the company were experiencing a busy period, and as a result, the original members of the demonstration team were changed; the presumably skilled and motivated individuals were required to "man the pumps". Instead, two other workers, obviously not considered high flyers, were spared even under the busy conditions the factory was experiencing.

Both of them were in their early twenties, unmarried, and at that time living at home. With the permission of their parents, they were to visit London for a week, staying in a hotel. Neither had stayed in a four-star hotel before, let alone seen the sights of the capital city.

Monday saw the girls being given a prepared course, and subsequently a totally revised second seminar. The development team's preconceptions of the knowledge of shop floor workers, and factory life were completely different from reality; the girls were accustomed to being directed as to what to do, and how and when to do it. This posed a paradoxical situation, as the software developed throughout the project assumed an empowered workforce, one that was eager, proactive and motivated to contribute and learn.

By Wednesday a significant culture change had occurred; the girls were actively making comments and positive contributions to the software interfaces and work practices. They were afforded the autonomy to customise their work environment and the development team members were keen to take on board their ideas and judgements.

During their stay, it became evident that both girls were very fed up with factory life, wanting instead to become a computer programmer and a nanny respectively. At the end of the week, both returned to their jobs until the Open Day demonstration, which they enjoyed immensely. Neither girl had realised previously what factory working conditions could be like, if organised in teams, or cells, supported by the tools to facilitate this way of working.

An interesting turn of events took place after a week of working with the BICC team in an environment that was conducive to teamwork, participation and involvement. Both girls' expectations, on joining the factory some years previously, had been to continue to work there until marriage beckoned. Within six weeks of the open day, both had resigned in search for a better and more liberating working life. They had requested more responsibility but had been refused.

Karen went to work for IBM as a computer operator for six months, while finishing her evening training course in IT, and then managed to obtain a position as a systems analyst in a small computer company. Jill successfully got a position as a nanny in a large household, and several months later decided to travel the world. She now works in the public relations field in Australia.

At this juncture, it must be stressed that the training week and open day were not necessarily directly responsible for the dramatic changes in life style that took place for Jill and Karen. It would seem a tremendous coincidence, however, that these two individuals had changed so radically, whereas their peers are still in the same factory, with more or less the same responsibilities. The time spent with the BICC team was an important factor; exactly how important we shall never know.

Raising the awareness of workers is not without risk. Awareness may lead to alienation and restlessness. For some managers, to awaken the workforce to the unsatisfactory nature of their normal working conditions is unhelpful, even subversive.

## THE CASE OF TOM

Tom was a skilled lathe operator in his early thirties and worked in an area of the factory adjoining the one where the open day demonstration cell was being operated. During the open day preparations he visited a number of times, being inquisitive by nature and keen to understand what was going on. His nature was friendly, and he had an easy-going manner.

The problem of who would lead the first cell arose during the formation of the demonstration cell system, and the General Manager and Works Director were both uncertain as to who would be appropriate. Subsequently, several training courses were run at the site during the demonstration week and at the weekend. At the time, there appeared to be a great supervisory vacuum in the organisation: a lot of potential and expectations were being built, yet no one saw where they would fit in the new order of things. The whole shop floor tended to go around in circles, with management unclear on implementing the new changes.

The crunch point came when the General Manager admitted to the problem of not being able to find a suitable manager of the cell, and asked for ideas. When Tom was suggested, it came as a complete surprise: he had not even been noticed! Within two months, Tom was trained, promoted and positive to the new work practices being implemented. He was pleased and motivated by the mechanism of empowerment and what that meant to his immediate work environment, and to those he interacted with around him. During this transition, his new peer group welcomed him in his expanded role and he progressed quickly, finally being given responsibility for all the systems on the shop floor.

Financial pressures, the very same pressures that forced through the initial change, eventually resulted in the factory being relocated further north. Tom was offered a contract to ensure the smooth transition of the systems from one factory to the other. Culture in the new factory was not the same, however, and there existed very limited training and enthusiasm for the new approach: the empowerment ethos had not yet been transferred to the new site. Consequently, Tom found alternative employment elsewhere.[*]

As is the case in many instances, the lessons to be learnt are painfully clear in retrospect. The process of thinking, reflection and discussion, which leads to the

---

[*]Names have been changed to preserve anonymity.

conclusion that an organisation's employees are its greatest asset, is far from a hollow marketing exercise, and is one that all organisations should undertake.

# Levels of Empowerment

It is important to stress that there is no single approach that is ideal in every industry, company, function or situation. The impact of empowerment techniques is almost impossible to quantify. Like most things in management, the ideal form of empowerment is very much dependent upon circumstances.

Two academics, Bowen and Lawler (Bowen and Lawler 1992), have worked extensively in the field. They describe three categories of involvement, as opposed to an either–or approach to control versus empowerment, namely suggestion involvement, job involvement and high involvement; these they describe as follows.

## SUGGESTION INVOLVEMENT

Because it is only a small step away from control, many would argue that this option does not merit the term empowerment. Although employees are encouraged to contribute ideas, their daily work routines do not change and they are empowered only to recommend, not to implement.

McDonalds Restaurants is a follower of this approach. Its Big Mac, McBLT and Egg McMuffin dishes were suggested by employees, as was an improved method to wrap burgers, preventing thumb prints. Interestingly, Florida Power and Light, winners of the Deming Quality Award, define empowerment in suggestion involvement terms.

## JOB INVOLVEMENT

Involving extensive job design, this level of involvement allows employees to use a spectrum of skills. The approach is often typical of a team-based environment that allows considerable freedom in deciding how to complete necessary work. Subsequently, employees in this environment require training to deal with the added complexity of their responsibilities. Supervisors are reorientated towards supporting the shop floor, rather than directing it. This level of empowerment affects the workers' immediate environment, but does not impact the higher-level strategic decisions, including organisational structures, power, and the allocation of rewards. These are still the responsibility of senior management.

Within a UK DTI-sponsored project (BESTMAN; see Appendix 4), a UK-based company initiated a job-involvement-based empowerment initiative with their shift managers, known as "cell leaders". Cell leaders were given enhanced management responsibilities and were encouraged to involve themselves in areas not immediately under their responsibility, hence cross-fertilising ideas and knowledge. Training was deemed essential, and cell leaders were continually educated in key issues.

The company operated a 112-hour week, with three shifts and hence three different cell leaders. The lack of communication was having repercussions on critical areas. The organisation effectively operated as three different factories, and diffusing ideas between these "factories" was essential for results. The empowerment of these cell leaders, as well as other organisational changes, resulted in on-time delivery (a critical factor in their business) improving from 58% to 84% in only 9 months.

## HIGH INVOLVEMENT

Employees are involved in not just how to do their own jobs, but also in the whole organisation's performance. Virtually every aspect of the organisation is different from that of a control-orientated one. Information on business performance is shared horizontally across the organisation, as well as up and down the (now delayered) structure. Employees develop extensive skills in teamwork, problem solving and business operations. Workers participate in work-unit management decisions, and there is profit sharing as well as employee ownership.

High involvement programmes are expensive to implement, and this technique is relatively undeveloped, but there are examples of success. Federal Express, whose company motto is "people, service and profits", began a company-wide effort to convert to a team-based environment and organised its thousand clerical workers into teams of 5–10 people. These teams were given the authority and training to manage themselves, and helped the organisation to cut customer service problems, such as lost packages, by 13% in 1989. In 1990, Federal Express became the first service organisation to win the Malcolm Baldrige Quality Award (see Chapter 8).

Rank Xerox has also experimented with high involvement empowerment techniques. Vernon Zelmer, Rank Xerox's UK Managing Director, states, "we have basically told the teams to run the business ... important decisions are gradually being devolved to work groups". The director of customer service sees no practical limit on the authority devolved and says, "we are looking into ways that teams could eventually carve up their own salary increases, for example".

Both the latter examples were relatively recent, and do not have this level of empowerment throughout the whole organisation. Perhaps the most interesting and sustained example of high involvement is the Brazilian-based company Semco (discussed below), which has pioneered this form of working (Semler 1993, *Financial Times* 25 June 1993, *Guardian* 28 September 1993).

## Case Study: SEMCO – São Paulo, Brazil

High-involvement empowerment techniques are few and far between, and most organisations only operate on small isolated pockets, usually with astonishing success. This is not exclusively the case, however. Semco, based in Brazil, has been making pumps, dishwashers, cooling units and other industrial equipment under the leadership of Ricardo Semler, who was handed control of the company 14 years ago. Since that time, Semco has earned the reputation of being the fastest-growing Latin American company, with sales increasing sixfold and profits soaring by 500% to nearly $3 million. Productivity has risen sevenfold and the company is free of debt.

This alone might have explained the international attraction the company enjoys, from executives originating from some of the largest multinationals. However, it is not until the corporate culture, behaviour, hierarchy and work environment is examined that the reasons for the attention Semco and Semler receive becomes clearer.

Semler has turned traditional Tayloristic ideals on their head, and rather than workers being the dispensable cog in the corporate machine they are afforded true democracy; the worker is the one who drives the company forward. Some facets of the "Semler effect" include the following:

- Workers fix their own salary levels. It is not in the interest of workers to pitch their next year's increase too high, for fear of pricing themselves out of the department's budget. Furthermore, there are no controls over expenses or business travel.
- The performances of superiors are regularly reviewed by employees. Managers, including Semler himself, have to be rated anonymously by employees, by means of ratings on a scale of 1 to 100. Managers who consistently underperform are removed. Nobody has to spell out the obvious fact that the manager has lost the capacity to lead.
- Workers, who also have a stake in the company, elect their own boss. As Semler states, "asking subordinates to choose future bosses seems a sensible way of stopping accidents before they are promoted".
- Workers come and go as they like, and work the hours they deem necessary. Employees do not abuse the responsibility of controlling their own destiny. Co-workers and peer pressure prevent too much deviation.
- Workers decide on how much profit to share and reinvest. The profit-sharing scheme, up to 25% of profits, is determined by employees.
- Many employees are encouraged to work from home, or establish their own companies. At any one time, up to two-thirds of the people in Semco buildings are not directly employed, but are former employees now consulting.
- The Fordist assembly line has been abandoned and employees re-organise their factories to maximise their own productivity.
- The pyramidal structure and related power symbols have disappeared;

there are no secretaries and reserved parking spaces. Seven layers of management have been shed over the years.

At first glance this anarchic corporate behaviour appears to have the makings for potential chaos, yet the company has prospered and continues to do so in a harsh environment of hyperinflation. Despite this economic climate, Semco still manages to export almost 23% of its output. Semler urges organisations to take the leap of faith in giving up control, and states that the source of power in an organisation is information. Semco have brought all information out into the open: for instance, all employees have access to expenses and payroll data for the company.

Semler, much like Deming, has faith in the integrity, responsibility and capacity of the individual. He does not use an office or a desk. Semler does not believe in running the organisation by numbers, and claims that "Financial numbers are not an adequate indication of what is happening.... I feel closest to the company when I am talking to people."

Semco perhaps epitomises the act of empowerment with startling and success-ful results. Is this a one-off freak case, or a glimpse into how future companies could be, and perhaps should be, run?

# IT and the Shop Floor

Approximately 97% of your people are creative, vigorous, loyal, committed, caring and energetic: except for the eight hours they work for you.

*Tom Peters,* In Search of Excellence *(Peters 1982)*

Tom Peters's comments are interesting, not only because he is regarded as the world's leading management guru, but in part because he has a degree in civil engineering as well as a business doctorate. Poor industrial performance is too often attributed to the lack of trained engineers, but Peters argues that establish-ing more training programmes are not the whole answer to the problem. This conclusion was also reached by Björn Gustavsen when evaluating projects supported by the Swedish Work Environment Fund. The secret, Peters argues, is in empowerment.

A fundamental difference between people and machines is that people have a psychological environment, motivation or empowerment, for which an adequate physical environment is a necessary condition. The issue of human empower-ment has been largely ignored, by both the technologists and the human-factors community, especially in respect of the design of technology. Unless people are empowered, they do not function as a complement to technology, and this is an important criterion when designing technology. If their work does not represent a challenge then users will not use their flexibility, experience, skills or judgement, and, most importantly, they will not learn or assume responsibility. Peters believes that shop floor staff can be entrusted with far more responsibility than they are usually given; he suggests:

*"Just walk around and ask them what they do in their spare time.... You'll find that a high proportion of them have skilled hobbies, part-time jobs and community roles and responsibilities."*

People differ significantly from machines, and when they are forced to function like machines they sense that they are being used inefficiently and considered as stupid. People cannot tolerate being used in this way and, overtly or covertly, they resist and rebel against it. Empowering the workforce acts as a catalyst for new ideas and suggestions, and employees are as likely as customers to produce ideas for new products. The idea for the Sony Walkman or 3M's Post-it notes did not come from customers but were ideas developed, albeit accidentally, by the workforce.

The general opinion that it can be easier to see the payoffs from different management practices in the manufacturing sector, when this is compared with the service sector, is no longer relevant. A study of the companies in the Fortune 1000 in the US suggested that service companies tended to use significantly fewer employee involvement practices when compared with manufacturing companies. In the past, this characteristic could be attributed to the increased global competition faced by the manufacturing sector, which highlighted the inadequacies of the Tayloristic work paradigm. Over the past decade, however, the differences between sectors have been blurred, as service competition has increased and companies have access to increasingly sophisticated methods of tracking service quality.

Empowerment is equally applicable in all industries, including manufacturing, service and voluntary organisations. In Peters's book *Liberation Management* (Peters 1992) he quotes Cable News Network's profits of $167 million on revenues of $479 million. The essence of the founder Ted Turner's secret, Peters believes is "in finding terrific people, then getting out of their way". Importantly, Turner's attitude is mirrored throughout the organisation and it enables CNN personnel, at even junior levels, to take instant decisions about covering news stories. As service businesses begin to embrace empowerment techniques, much can be learnt from the manufacturing sector, which has been using quality circles, self-managed teams and participation groups for some time.

# A New Structure

Clinging on to established management techniques for decades has resulted in companies still harbouring outdated attitudes, and fostering a more human-centred attitude has far reaching consequences. A time-honoured way to gain power is by empire building – the acquisition of subordinates. When there is not enough work for them to do, as is the eventual case, they justify their position by creating unnecessary tasks for one another. Hence each rank of management tends to form another rank below it, continually inserting further, less productive, layers of supervision between the top decision makers and the shop floor – that elusive place where the real work of serving the customer actually gets done.

A balanced, empowered organisation can only be achieved in the context of new organisational structures. Organisations that have succeeded in implementing a more empowered workforce have inverted their pyramidal hierarchies, and senior managers are seen as coaches whose role is to counsel rather than issue orders. These organisations consist of teams, project groups and taskforces rather than departmental empires. The idea is not a new one (as further discussed in Chapter 8); Deming constantly emphasises co-operation throughout his philosophy; as he states many times, managers should play the role of coach, not cop. Not surprisingly, empowered companies also enjoy a fruitful and successful quality programme.

Although companies may not start out with empowerment as a goal, when levels of management are removed and time to market and other factors compressed, they end up with it. You cannot run a delayered organisation along human-centred lines by Tayloristic command and control methods. Harnessing the drive, ingenuity and power of people is central to re-engineering processes, and the people route is more timely, simpler, and in the long term, more cost-effective.

## THE BIG PICTURE

President Kennedy asked a man carrying out some patently menial task at Cape Canaveral, America's space launch site, what he was doing. "I'm helping to put a man on the moon", was the reply.

*Financial Times, 5 May 1993*

To win commitment from their employees, employers need to convey the full picture of the meaning and contribution of their jobs. Even routine work can be rewarding if employees understand that their efforts, however insignificant, make a difference. Lessons can be learnt from the voluntary sector, where fund-raisers are willing to spend hours licking envelopes in an effort to help their favourite charity. Participants believe in the values, mission and broader approach of the charity organisation. Professor Rosabeth Moss Kanter, of Harvard Business School, states (Kanter 1989) that

*"... people used to work to get a title, now they work to achieve a result ... rewarding people for their contribution frees them from the need to get promoted in order to get more money."*

These very attributes, or the lack of them, are key to the failure of many empowerment programmes. Kanter argues that traditional pay structures often consist of underpayment for overperformance in the early years of one's career, and overpayment for underperformance in the later ones.

## THE BIG MISTAKE

A mistake is an event the full benefit of which has not been turned to your advantage.

*Ed Land, Founder and President of Polaroid*

Mistakes are regarded as an important learning process, and an essential element of our childhood development. One would assume that this would be true throughout our professional lives, yet in the corporate learning process most companies are reluctant to acknowledge them. Indeed, British corporate culture encourages employees to hide their mistakes, and as a result the learning opportunities are lost. Similar errors are replicated by other individuals, ultimately damaging reputation and profitability.

Many would see these characteristics as typical of the British tendency for short termism and a low-trust culture. The example of Hoover's disastrous marketing campaign epitomises the fact that big mistakes cannot be hidden for long. An idea to boost sales, by offering two free flights to Europe or America to any customer spending a minimum of £100 on Hoover products, at first seemed an excellent promotional drive. However, marketing executives had miscalculated the strength of demand and the tenacity of customers, which eventually made the campaign hugely more expensive than anticipated. The initial mistakes were exacerbated by a series of further mistakes, eventually costing the parent company, Maytag, $30 million to cover the unexpected cost of the promotion. Subsequently the European president and two senior executives were fired.

The lessons are clear in retrospect, yet the ideology of a balanced learning organisation, allowing employees greater autonomy to manage their own work and aspirations, is not common. A study by Keith Grint, of Templeton College, Oxford, confirms this view. The study looks at the processes whereby organisations displace responsibility for decisions and managerial problems. His comments shed some light on the issue (Grint 1993):

*"In British organisations there are no rewards for being the bearer of bad news. Managers who make it to the top are usually those who tell the managers above them what they want to hear. Even those organisations that have tried to introduce empowerment do not give managers and employees lower down sufficient rein to*

*enable them to make mistakes and then learn from them. Errors which should be a powerful means of learning, are not."*

An important element of a quality management approach requires a focus upon positive acceptances of change. As Deming states, workers are afraid of reporting problems or suggesting improvements because of their fear of "rocking the boat" and subsequently losing their jobs. Management should foster an environment that drives out fear.

Errors are not necessarily the fault of the individual. In most cases they are caused by a flaw in the systems or processes by which the company operates. Unless acknowledged, the problem cannot be addressed and the potential for further mistakes still exists.

Peter Edwards, the Managing Director of Talkland, a UK-based cellular telephone company that turned a £1 million loss per week to profit, encouraged employees to play a part and state what was going wrong. He states (*Times* 19 August 1993):

*"What happens in most companies is a process of data sanitation. Bad news and mistakes are filtered out by people reporting up through the organisation. The result is that people at the top don't know what's going wrong. The only way to find out is to get people to tell you what mistakes are being made by the company, and to give them the freedom to correct them."*

# Potential Problems: Opening Pandora's Box

Although managers and senior management believe that empowerment is vital to the improvement of business efficiency and quality, many are worried that empowerment could open up Pandora's box. Problems originate from confusion and inadequate commitment to the programmes set in motion. Some common issues include the following:

- There is confusion between empowerment and delegation. Empowerment is more than just pushing responsibility down an organisation, and potential improvements cannot be realised if people are expected to take control over work when they do not possess the necessary skills and competences. Delegation often simply consists of direction with very little autonomy. Empowerment involves support through continuous training and education, elements that are vital to its success. The learning process should be promoted across the organisation.
- Power conscious managers are not committed to the programme and are misled about losing authority. To improve motivation and performance, the power equation has to be readdressed. The new type of organisation is

one that should share power; this does not necessarily mean surrendering it. Jack Furrer, director of management education at Ciba-Geigy, reflects from their experience in empowering the workforce: "People still need direction.... Managers need to create an environment which suits both themselves and their employees" (Furrer 1992). The balance between autonomy and direction varies according to the individual, and empowering the workforce sometimes requires boundaries.

- Much is dependent on implementation, and every employee must be actively involved in the process. Many UK companies have started their change processes with unnecessarily grand abstractions, rather than specific challenges that are easily understood, like customer service. The danger lies in creating expectation when nothing happens.

- Many companies will opt for the top-down approach, the idea being that all changes should be decided at the top of the company and then filtered down. Instead, a top-bottom-middle approach is more effective, according to Kinsley Lord, a consultancy specialising in the management of change. The initiative for changing small-scale practices is handed directly to local teams. These local initiatives blossom, and middle managers then need help in learning how to encourage and facilitate efforts, rather than frustrate it.

- Too often, the threat of middle management losing their jobs is a real one and in many cases this should not necessarily be the case. As power and responsibility is devolved downwards from middle management, existing middle managers should be afforded new roles and responsibilities originating from upper management. The top-down approach is successful in empowering workers at the lower level, but does not provide for the middle manager; information and responsibilities, and hence power, are still hypocritically withheld at the top.

These are some of the reasons why empowerment programmes have failed in the past. In the majority of successful implementations, companies have introduced empowerment techniques as one element of an organisation-wide programme of process re-engineering.

## THE END OF AUTHORITARIAN RULE

The psychology of control is the key underpinning of Tayloristic rule, and has been the dominant concept for decades. It is not surprising that managers experience problems when they attempt to shift their focus to a more democratic and empowered workforce.

Too many managers use new technology to control, an ancient resort of the failed leader. Much like the hereditary rulers before them, control is for them a fail-safe system to guard against the frailties of their authority. This attitude is not far off from that of the feudal kings who would take hostages from a noble person's family, in case they should cause trouble, or fail to pay their taxes.

For Taylor and other American managers at the turn of the century, much of the labour that fuelled the industrial revolution constituted of immigrants with low levels of education and only a basic understanding of the English language. It was productive to show them one best way of working. The managers at that time had a better understanding of the worker's job than the worker did.

Today the situation is somewhat different, however, with employees more educated and willing to learn; they don't park their brains outside the company building. Workers today know more about their jobs than the managers do, and instead of using basic tools they have command over complex computers. They need to be able to use judgement and understand the wider strategic objectives of their company environment. Correspondingly, the relationships nurtured by managers with their workers need to change to reflect this.

The worker of the 1990s is motivated by objectives that differ from those of several decades ago, and it is critical for management to understand this, yet it is difficult to actually contemplate what motivation really means. Is it addressing what an individual needs from their working environment, apart from just money?

Mayo, Maslow, Herzberg, Skinner and many others have conducted much research on the needs and motivations of individuals. Need theories are loaded with dangerous associations, and, as Handy points out, implicit in them is the idea that anyone who can satisfy these needs has some influence over the behaviour of the person with the need (Handy 1988).

# The Hawthorne Effect

When considering empowerment techniques, the work of Elton Mayo as an observer of the experiments at the Western Electric Hawthorne Works in Chicago is often cited by managers to explain sudden rises in worker productivity.

From the mid-1920s to the early 1940s, the Western Electric Company conducted a programme of experiments into human behaviour at their Hawthorne Works, which employed over 40 000 workers. Over a period of two years, groups of workers were monitored, and conditions of work were progressively changed. Group bonus incentive schemes were introduced, rest pauses implemented, free snacks and refreshments offered and a shorter working week was advocated.

In the twelfth period, all privileges were removed and then restored in the next. During all of these periods, the hourly output rose, even during the deprived twelfth one. Each change had resulted in measurable enhancements in workforce productivity, even when the system was returned to the start conditions. It was assumed that after a period of time the novelty of being the centre of attention would wear off, and productivity levels would begin to taper off. This became known as the Hawthorne effect.

Implications of the experiment have been summarised by managers, who have stated that it is not what is measured that is important – it is the act of measurement that creates the improvement. Managers have extrapolated the implications of the effect to mean that any new workplace changes would only result in short-term gains.

There is much contention over Mayo's Hawthorne research, and certainly the two definitive reports that were written up are difficult to follow and lengthy. Synopses are often subject to distortion and partisanship. However, of note is the work by W. J. Dickson and F. J. Roethlisberger (Dickson and Roethlisberger 1939), who wrote up the experiments that were carried out at the plant. Their conclusions centre on the point that workers are not motivated by financial rewards (bonus incentive schemes), but more importantly by a comfortable and supportive environment that encourages supervisors to be more centred towards the needs of the workers.

Richard Gillespie has researched the histories of the experiments; he begs to differ from the well-known and cited interpretation of the Hawthorne effect, and states that there is ample evidence to suggest that workers "fixed" their output by adjusting their working rates: first overperforming and then subsequently underperforming the next day, in order to reach a mutually accepted output for the week. This view is also argued by Rose (Rose 1988).

A researcher's note about a supervisor suggests that the Hawthorne effect has more than the one dimension of monitoring groups of workers. It states that a supervisor "probably had more to do with breaking down the barriers in the employee–supervisor relationship than any other factor ... he injected a sense of spirit in the group ... encouraging them to call everyone by their first name". This behaviour of a supervisor in the plant is contrary to that suggested by Mayo (Mayo 1933).

The well-accepted conclusions (i.e. the importance of measurement) of the Hawthorne studies by management are not necessarily as clear-cut as they may originally have seemed. They have influenced control strategies for decades and, in some cases, reinforce an authoritarian way of thinking, whereas further, more in-depth research indicates otherwise. The studies have been the basis for justifying other research projects akin to the Hawthorne experiments, and these studies can be said to be as the beginnings of the "human relations" movement.

# Abraham Maslow and B. F. Skinner

## ABRAHAM MASLOW

Maslow's approaches to motivation have had a profound impact on human-resource management. The organisational application of Maslow's theories on individuals' needs and motivation suggests that people's needs operate in an ascending hierarchy. With Maslow's model, people must be moved through the levels, not leap from bottom to top. Maslow's five categories form a hierarchy, outlined in Figure 5.1, in which basic needs are satisfied before safety needs, etc.

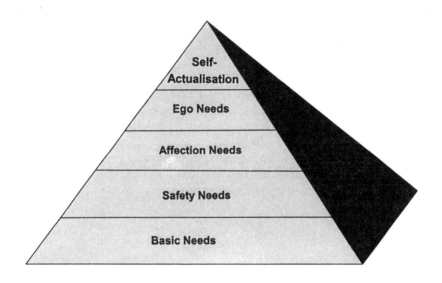

*Figure 5.1    Maslow's hierarchy of needs*

- *Physiological or basic needs.* These are needs that people must satisfy just to stay alive (i.e. food and drink), regardless of tomorrow's problems or promises.
- *Security or safety needs.* These are concerned with self-protection and the desire for security for the future.
- *Belonging or affection needs.* These reflect people's need to give and receive friendship by having friends and belonging to social groups.
- *Esteem or ego needs.* People need to become independent, to acquire possessions and to receive praise.
- *Self-actualisation needs.* These needs are concerned with self-fulfilment, being creative and using one's capabilities to the fullest.

Maslow proposes that people can be categorised into pigeon-holes, according to the highest level of their needs. His theories can be read to imply that management is motivated by power, money and status: extrinsic incentives influence the individual's behaviour, which is reminiscent of the old corporate structure.

## B. F. SKINNER

Enthusiasts for the behavioural psychology of B. F. Skinner have tried to apply his work to the industrial context. Skinner was convinced that human behaviour could be controlled and conditioned, and that workplaces could then be conceived and mechanistically engineered. His research centred on "the science of behaviour", "operant behaviour", "the control of men" and conditioning using deprivation and punishment. His work and ideas were brought to fruition with the publication of his findings in the mid-twentieth century.

Skinner believed that for workers to be motivated they had to be rewarded for the right behaviour, and derived his supposedly scientific proofs from starving rats and pigeons, and then displaying that they can be conditioned to do simple tasks; pigeons were taught to dance for their food (Skinner 1953).

In the same manner, Skinner held, humans could be conditioned for greater productivity, by extrinsic incentives. However, Skinner's theory negates the values of empowerment; if workers are continually attempting to please their superiors, unhealthy and unproductive competition and rivalries form between individuals. Fearing mistakes, workers are in fact resistant to increased responsibility, and hence seek to delegate decisions upwards.

# Teamworking 6

## Introduction

Teams, and teamworking within organisations, have attracted considerable attention. It is presumed that the introduction of team structures will have a beneficial result. This perception may have much to do with the single-minded obsession with emulating the successful Japanese example of work organisation, without a full appreciation of the changes that need to be made in order to achieve effective results in an environment outside a collectivist culture.

Teamwork has made significant impacts on productivity within the manufacturing and service sectors, and the benefits have been numerous. The technique has been utilised as an element of greater change, working hand in hand with empowerment and business process re-engineering. New advancements in technology have given birth to "Groupware": a concept that embraces software to provide an infrastructure that supports teamworking.

This chapter explores advances in group collaborative working and introduces a human-centred groupworking software tool.

The team concept is often mentioned in the context of empowerment; the two almost seem to go hand in hand, tapping into the underutilised resources of employees. The attention to teamwork may have been unnecessary, because nearly all of us work with other people and are interdependent in the sense that we interact with colleagues, friends and peers; there has been an obsession with the postwar Japanese economic miracle and with obtaining the secret of perceived Japanese success.

The Japanese originate from a complex and collectivist culture, however, and naturally perform in groups or teams, while in the Anglo-Saxon hemisphere individualism is king and individual effort is rewarded and encouraged. No matter how much teamwork activity occurs, in our culture the results are attributed to a single name, and organisations tend to foster this attitude.

In most democratic organisations there exists an inevitable tension between collective and individual needs. Deming's solution to this is that conflicting individual goals should be eliminated; too many companies encourage conflict through the establishment of individual goals, implicitly or explicitly. Traditional organisational structures have hardly helped to alleviate this situation.

# Teams: Flavour of the Month

The flattening of the managerial pyramid, and the shedding of hierarchy coupled with increasingly empowered employees, appear to be the means by which organisations are able to survive in business in the 1990s.

Accountability and decision making need to be devolved to multi-functional teams that can cross traditional functional boundaries. Changing societal and individual values are beginning to filter through to corporate thinking; we are beginning to see the end of the individualistic mentality that dominated the 1980s, with performance-related pay and the cult of individual progression. There is an emphasis on collectivistic values and more team-based approaches to meet new challenges, and the goal is to sustain team-based attitudes in newly re-engineered processes. Teams can help to create the social structure for the effective dissemination of values and culture, but organisations have lacked this framework and have relied instead on hierarchical and vertical control systems.

For many practitioners, teams seem to offer an automatically egalitarian and democratic organisational culture. It would be naïve to assume that all pigs are equal, however. Teams are not necessarily applicable in all functions of an organisation; the key to success is identifying those areas that will benefit from a team approach. Typically, these areas in which job roles place a need for high interdependence upon the various individuals who perform them.

## WHAT IS A TEAM?

A team is a group of people sharing common goals and purposes, with each individual bringing expertise and knowledge to the collective whole, and much research has been conducted on what ingredients constitute a good one. Belbin (Belbin 1981) made a study of the mix of personal characteristics in a group, and concluded that a group of the brightest people did not necessarily constitute the brightest team. Indeed, studying the Apollo space team, he concluded that the collective IQ of the team was often lower than individual IQs of its members; he termed this the Apollo syndrome.

Eight roles that are needed in a group have been abridged from Belbin's book (p. 78), and are listed in Table 6.1.

Table 6.1    Belbin's team roles

| | Team roles |
|---|---|
| The chairman | No more than ordinary in terms of brilliance or creativity, the chairman is a good judge, who is focused and balanced. |
| The plant | The intellectual who is introverted and possesses imagination. They can disregard details or protocol. |
| The company worker | The organiser who is practical: an administrator turns ideas into tasks. |
| The shaper | The highly strung and dynamic leader who is always ready for the challenge: can be provocative and insensitive. |
| The finisher | An orderly and conscientious individual who worries about small things. |
| The resource investigator | The enthusiastic extrovert who brings in new ideas and contacts although may not be involved after that. |
| The monitor–evaluator | The necessary critic who has the ability to spot flaws but does not inspire or motivate others. |
| The teamworker | The sociable and liked personality who promotes the team spirit and is committed. |

Belbin's approach and framework can be useful as a starting point, but there is much confusion about what a team actually is, and whether teams are necessary and appropriate throughout an organisation. We may say that common purposes will unite a group of individuals working together, but it is only a high level of interdependence that will transform that group into a true team.

## TEAM TYPES

A whole plethora of different "types" of teams can exist and flourish within organisations, with each type possessing different characteristics, goals and interactions within the organisation. The work of Higgs and Rowland provides a useful and workable framework classifying the types into four distinct quadrants, as outlined in Figure 6.1 (Higgs and Rowland 1992).

As well as the formally constituted team, in which a group of workers is brought together in an official sense, we should note the existence of the informal team, in which individuals combine naturally, identifying with each other and sharing ideas and resources. With formal teams, membership and goals are established by management, whereas informal teams have only implicitly recognised accountabilities and are more difficult to "document" and guide.

With the organisational work environment becoming more dynamic, there is an increasing need for individuals who are able to work with other individuals from cross-functional areas. The teams so built exist to achieve certain set goals, usually within a finite period of time. In contrast, certain areas of the work environment require individuals who need to work together on a continuous basis, for common goals that unite the members over a longer period of time. We may thus define the other two dimensions of teams as permanent and temporary.

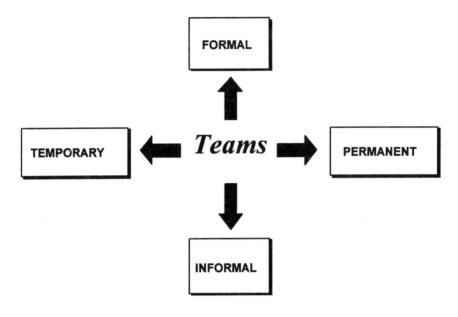

*Figure 6.1    A quadrant of team types*

# Groupware

Groupware is a term coined to embrace the collection of software programs designed for people working in teams. Together with the appropriate hardware, it provides an infrastructure to co-ordinate individuals in a group. With the increasing proliferation of computer networks, and with personal computers easily connected together, many companies already have the potential to share greater information than they do. Groupware facilitates this new dimension.

Groupware goes back to the 1960s, and the work of Douglas Engelbart at the Stanford Research Institute, exploring the use of computers to support human intellect. His On-Line System contained many advanced features that are available, albeit in a more advanced format, in many of today's groupware products. Engelbart is credited with the invention of the mouse pointer, and was a pioneer of computer-supported teams.

Many of the early ideas were held back by the lack of hardware at economic prices. Today, buildings are wired for networking, and hardware is a common commodity. The market for groupware products has flourished, and many companies are realising the potential of true teamworking, through the increasing empowerment of employees and the flattening of pyramidal organisational structures.

Groupware is one element of the newer initiative in business process re-engineering. The introduction of the software and hardware inherently creates a change in working culture, including new work practices. The introduction of the technology changes the potential power balance within a business organisation, some of whose members will perceive gains and others losses. What is required, before one is able to take full advantage of what groupware can offer, is understanding, practice and reflection. One has to only think back to those individuals who would not leave a message on an answer machine 15 years ago; today we see some that are intimidated by the advent of a teleconferencing camera. The technology continues to advance and work practices need to change in tandem: workers need to adapt to using new tools.

# Challenging Orthodoxy

Groupware, by its very nature, challenges the vertical hierarchy prevalent in many established organisations, and interferes with the political forces at play in the company. The enhanced communication that groupware advocates, if it is to be utilised to some degree of its potential, undermines the power relationship that exists in vertically hierarchic organisations; managers lose the easy control of information that constituted a significant element of their personal power.

Let us take the most elemental form of groupware functionality: electronic mail. Should a manager pass only certain elements of information "down the line" to his subordinates, there is the possibility of many repercussions, such as contradictory decisions by subordinates, based on incomplete information. The message may reach the subordinate through another channel, without having first been tampered with; the ease of disseminating information electronically throws open many communication channels, crossing functions and departments. The old hierarchical policy of the manager preparing information in a format that can be understood by those lower down is not so necessary in the contemporary organisation. Those who rely on these policies to maintain their power cannot win.

## DIFFERENT SPHERES OF KNOWLEDGE

Evaluating the benefits of groupware and introducing it has proved to be a difficult and elusive process. The term is often coupled with computer-supported collaborative working (CSCW); the two involve the same processes. The emphasis on work is an important one, in that the technology promotes a more democratic workplace, and the work of Scandinavian researchers in this area is illustrative (Bjerknes and Ehn 1987). Such research has been followed by a rapid proliferation of the technology; indeed, all too often the introduction of new technology has not been preceded by research, because of the pressure of rapid technological advance. CSCW packages are now routinely available to non-specialist business users.

The successful implementation and use of groupware demands a fusion of different spheres of knowledge and discipline:

- Social, political, motivational and psychological;
- Human–computer interface issues;
- The use of knowledge-based systems, expert systems and artificial intelligence;
- Technical: distributed systems and communication technologies.

Each sphere has a varying role to play, depending on the extent and complexity of the groupware solution being considered. The fusion is still evolving, but the tacit acceptance of the need, by those concerned, has brought meaningful debates between computer scientists and social scientists. What use is groupware, if there are no groups to use the technology?

The promise of CSCW software is that in its evolved form, the output will be smoothly functioning project teams, with experts from different functionalities fused by a common purpose and relying on the underlying technology.

# A Question of Language

Different forms of groupware pose critical questions about the use of language. At a relatively simple level of groupware, we can use electronic mail (email); a little more complex is the use of video conferencing. As we move up the ladder of complexity, other forms of our ability to communicate come into play (verbal, written and so on). With real-time conferencing, one can glean non-verbal information; at the email level we only have the written word.

Now contrast email with the use of the telephone: the latter involves non-formal communication and one receives an instant reply; there is shared understanding, implicit and explicit. Not so with email. The act of putting our thoughts and requests in a formal memo focuses our attention on the language expressed, which can have very different meanings in varying cultural contexts. The response is not immediate, giving the sender time to reflect upon and refine what might have first been put forward as a reply.

English may be the international business language throughout the world, but it is not universally understood in the same context. For example, there are many different cultural deviations from the norm: in Italy one does not request, but invite (only the government can request), while Japanese culture does not advocate the declining of a request, because the Japanese are reluctant to appear to offend (Winograd and Flores 1988).

Through learning and experience, some users of groupware have gradually adapted to the technology and acquired the skills of the new culture, once the dimension of language has been considered.

# Group Working on the Factory Floor

The very idea of group work as an element of the manufacturing process runs against the ideas advocated by Taylor. Increasingly, organisations are using small teams, or cells. Ingersoll engineers have called this the "quiet revolution", since there has been a boom in the adoption of cell-based manufacture (Ingersoll 1982). Many ideas that are embedded in the group technology cell concept promised in the 1970s to be the panacea for resolving productivity and quality problems, but were never widely accepted. Twenty years on, the technology has matured and there is now overwhelming evidence of the widespread adoption of functions supporting autonomous, product-based cells.

Cells are self-contained business units within the overall organisation, and are fully responsible for their own operations; to other, upstream cells in the organisation they are suppliers and to those downstream they are customers. Moving different processes together requires employees, who were previously in different departments, to work more closely with each other. Getting started in cellular manufacturing requires a long-term commitment on the part of management, engineering and, importantly, the shop floor. Successful efforts have required little or no investment in equipment. Cells are in effect "factories within factories", each responsible for the control of all the resources needed to make its part of the product on time and at the right quality. Drucker (Drucker 1988) calls them "flotillas" as opposed to a "battleship", and states that modular organisations are vital to modern manufacturing, in which overall control of the factory is replaced by autonomous control at cell level.

To be effective, improvements should be radical. Colin New, Professor of Manufacturing Strategy at Cranfield School of Management (New 1992), believes that the challenge now is to transform companies by making major changes. He says, "Tinkering around with 10% improvements here and there is not good enough," He further warns that changes need to be made in the next few years, or "you will be out of business by the end of the nineties". In the area of quality failure, levels need to be reduced drastically; a well-cited example is a supplier of electric wiper motors to Nissan. Of the 12 million delivered to the car manufacturer, only 12 were faulty. Using cell methodology focuses more attention on quality, which becomes more critical because parts that used to sit in work-in-progress (WIP) inventories now go directly to the next process. The contribution of each employee assigned to the cell becomes more apparent.

# Implementing Cells

Cells increase the opportunity for achieving flexibility in product scheduling, as well as creating a feeling of ownership for employees. Several points have been highlighted for consideration in implementing a cellular manufacturing methodology:

- A well-defined objective and overall goal of the cell(s) should be identified.
- Management must make it clear to all employees that manufacturing cells receive their full support.
- Early involvement of employees is critical. A proposed layout should be made available for study and critique.
- Simulation should be used to fine-tune the cell design early and discuss the results.
- Lines of communication must be kept open. Topics should include those such as preventative maintenance, supplier information, inventory and sales information.
- If the work culture is appropriate, a group incentive should be established to reward employees for helping meet the cell's objectives.
- The scheme should not stop with individual cells. The entire factory should be focused to achieve a cohesive collection of cells within cells.
- Future products should be designed as far as possible with manufacturability in mind, utilising the benefits of cells as they become available.

The solution is not particularly simple, however. Ingersoll's respondents had made the largest allocation of funds for management and control systems, on average 24% of their budgets (Ingersoll 1982). Most underestimated the investment needed in people. The most successful 10% had invested 43% of their budgets in people and 29% in management and control systems. If cell techniques are to succeed, and business benefits are to be maximised then there must be accompanying changes in the organisational structure. Levels of management need to be reduced, and there has to be an increase in empowerment on the shop floor to facilitate quick decision making. From the very beginning, shop floor workers need to be involved as equal team members. People can improve profit growth by using intuition, perception, judgement and experience. Technology should be organised around people in a way that suits them and exploits their skills. The focus must be on people working within and managing cells, not merely acting as progress chasers or machine loaders.

# Forming Cells into Business Units

Many organisations have already taken the step of accepting that they have to be organised into cells, or autonomous business units. Furthermore, when implementing these structures, one can learn from others' experiences. Three distinct levels of formation can be identified, some of which have been successfully addressed while the others require more elaborate thinking. The three levels of business unit formation are

1.  The plant level.
2.  Skill level.
3.  Psychological level.

## THE PLANT LEVEL

This level has had much scrutiny by academics and industry, and one can manually utilise group technology to build these units. As Figure 6.2 shows, formulating cells at the plant level usually entails the organisation of machines and associated equipment within geographically optimised groups, supporting process flows of the products to be produced. There are not many computer-based tools to assist in the formation of cells at a plant level in today's factories. However, the concept of identifying every product required, while simultaneously matching needs with machines and all the plant that these products are to be manufactured on, is relatively straightforward. It is then possible, using cluster analysis techniques, to create cells based round these identified concentrations. It was this need that gave birth to the ACiT tool (see p. 96), developed as an element of a research project sponsored by the European Commission.

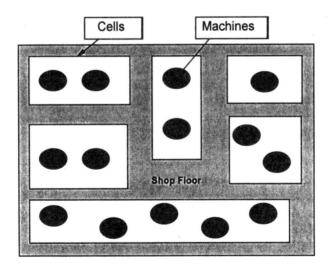

*Figure 6.2    Plant level business units*

## THE SKILL LEVEL

This level has been particularly poorly addressed. It has been assumed, on the whole, that once the mechanical plant has been formed into cells, then the appropriate people with the necessary skills will be available to man and effectively run the plant. This is very rarely the case, as can be seen with partners involved in project BESTMAN, especially DeVilbiss Ransburg and Temco (see Appendices 4 and 5), which both had to undertake extensive reskilling and educating initiatives.

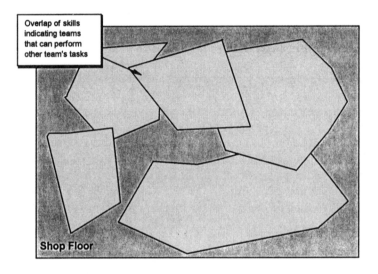

*Figure 6.3    Skill level business units*

Skills often overlap between workers and cells, as illustrated in Figure 6.3, and this wider base of available skill is often not used to its full potential. Currently, no known system or IT tool is in place to assist in the matching of skills to specific machines, or to formulate cells based upon specific skills.

## THE PSYCHOLOGICAL LEVEL

Again, this level is well covered. The Belbin studies, abridged earlier, are well known, and many psychometric measurements have been performed throughout the world, with some of these "measures" implemented on computer-based tools, so that the psychometric tests can be calculated. As Figure 6.4 illustrates, the psychological elements do not always map perfectly to the team, or cell, that has been built.

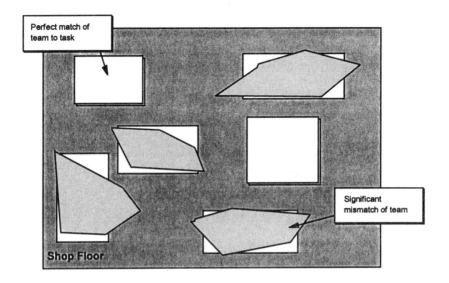

*Figure 6.4    Psychological business units*

In the current environment, it is essential for business units and processes to work effectively from day one, especially when cell structures are implemented. The plant has to be in the right place, at the right time, manned with the workers with the necessary competencies and skills. This is not enough, however; people also have to operate well and effectively within a team environment, *as* a team. The complexities of manually addressing all the parameters of plant, skill and psychological needs simultaneously are difficult at best, horrendous at worst. This is an area where computer-based decision tools can help tremendously.

It is to this end that tools are required: to help formulate prototype business units addressing all three levels: plant, skill and psychological. It is dangerous to focus on only one of the levels (usually the plant level). The ideal is not a solution generator, but more a suggestion maker, the premise upon which human-centred systems are built.

## THE BENEFITS

Many advantages, both tangible and intangible, of cellular manufacturing can be realised by firms of all sizes, no matter what their capital budgets are. The benefits of cellular manufacture can be impressive; the report published in 1982 by Ingersoll (Ingersoll 1982) cites 51% of UK engineering companies as using cells with over a fifth of the rest planning to, and only a mere 1.3% having abandoned the idea. Over half of the 200 companies reduced work in progress by 50% or more, and nearly 60% cut lead times by a similar amount. Some of the documented advantages include:

- Reduction in materials handling.
- Less scrap and improved quality.
- More stimulating work environment.
- Reduction/elimination of work-in-progress (WIP) storage areas.
- Improved scheduling.
- Greater flexibility.
- Reduced lot sizes.
- Reduced overall throughput time.

# IT in Cells

Cellular manufacture demands a variable amount of IT, and traditional computerised production management systems, such as Manufacturing Resource Planning (MRP II), can support the high-level planning functions of the company's business, but are inadequate for the operational control of the dynamic activities on the shop floor. The problem is that these key teams do not have access to appropriate decision support tools, simple gauging and scheduling systems that will take measurements from carefully chosen points on the product and print out a chart for them.

## THE ACiT TOOL

Appropriate Computer Integrated Manufacturing Technology (ACiT) is a software suite that was developed by BICC Technologies, initially as a planning and scheduling system. There is nothing unusual about that, but in its conception and development ACiT was a little different from most software projects.

The development of the system began during a project sponsored by the European Commission, namely ESPRIT 1199: Human Centred Computer Integrated Manufacturing (see Appendix 2 for more details). The UK element of the project was to produce a factory planning and scheduling tool to complement the overall strategy and theme of the project. The underlying philosophy was that a CIM system would be more economical and robust, with people directly in charge of the technology, rather than an unmanned system. This, at the time, went against the fashionable trend of attempting to produce systems that would operate in an unmanned "factory of the future".

The conceptualisation and ideas behind ACiT were developed a few years prior to the project. The development of ACiT is mentioned because it is presented as a tool that was developed to be used with a human-centred approach: it is human-centred IT. As is consistent with the approach, this is certainly not to say that this is the only way of using the tool; users are free to employ it as they please.

# THE BACKGROUND

During the 1970s and early 1980s, manufacturing operations were plagued by poor delivery, long lead times and high work in progress. Product innovation was stagnant and organisational change unpopular. This precipitated a surge in production methods based on new technology, and throughout the 1970s the message to industry from politicians, the manufacturing press and other learned bodies was to hasten the introduction of advanced manufacturing technology in the form of robotics, computer-numerical-controlled (CNC) machines and planning software utilising flexible manufacturing systems; this was seen as the panacea for the 1980s and 1990s.

The technological solutions were indeed outstanding, and many followed the technocrat's pipe-dream of increased efficiency and reduced costs through the deskilling and automation of the workforce. Unfortunately, although virtually all the systems achieved technical successes, competitiveness only improved marginally. This phenomenon was in line with the first author's own experience of working with medium-sized companies (total sales of approximately £200 million p.a.) that had made such investments.

The systems in use in such companies were not helping them to achieve the results they desired, and the performance measures in use were not beneficial to effective planning. Customers were no longer happy with 10 000 widgets in a single size, colour and shape. They now demanded 10 lots of a thousand, in various different permutations and combinations. Most advanced systems were not geared up for this, and not many workers within the companies had the technical skills to change.

It was a combination of these factors and others that led a team within the BICC Group to begin experimenting with an alternative approach. The goal was simple in its objectives: an IT-based tool that was simple to use, with an important management strategy implied: the emphasis on the tool meant trusting the experience and local knowledge of workers on the shop floor to achieve production targets. The tool was built to enable cells, or teams of workers, to realise results; the tool provided an infrastructure for cells to cross-fertilise and collaborate, which was important because production processes are very rarely linear. This was a very different approach compared with the highly automated solutions advocated at that time.

The way forward seemed to be to change organisational practice (putting a simple tool in the hand of the worker had a large cultural significance) and to use IT to handle "hard" work, such as routine and repetitive calculations. The human abilities of handling complex scenarios and suggesting improvements were clearly highlighted at the outset; this was an aspect that the tool was not expected to handle. A lot of personal judgement and needs were incorporated in a "mockup", or prototype; the seed grew into a more robust product. Fedback experience from use was absorbed, and the tool evolved. It was important to see the tool in a wide context of use; essentially, the wood had to be distinguished from the trees. Interaction with other systems in use was a desirable feature.

From day one, the tool was not expected to provide a "black-and-white" solution, but rather an approach that would work with the data provided and that would present "scenarios" that were easily adjusted and recalculated. The difficult job of deciding on the most appropriate course of action was left to the user, who would rely on experience and tacit judgement.

With hindsight, one may be tempted to say that all of this was doing the obvious, and that there was nothing new or revolutionary in it. What *was* revolutionary, however, was the linkage of some new ideas with older philosophies, balancing technology, organisation and people. The software *enabled* a human-centred way of working rather than attempting to *determine* it.

Today, ACiT continues to advance, with many other modules in the suite available, and still others being developed that employ the same approach. The strength of the tool lies in its ease of use, its low cost and its flexibility.

# Skill and Competence

## Skill: A Comparison

We are at the start of a new epoch, where efforts to reduce human work and knowledge are no longer seen as appropriate or profitable ways to advance businesses and economies. Technological advancement should have benefited society to a much greater extent than it has, and it is a lack of skilled human capital that has prevented this from happening. All too often organisations have ignored, or sometimes forgotten, the importance of a skilled and competent workforce. Even at the international level of the World Bank we can see a change of strategic direction, as development of human resources is recognised as a top priority.

Human-centred systems necessitate the effective and appropriate deployment of competence, tacit knowledge and skills, which address contemporary world trends in demographics and the needs for a qualified labour pool. HCS provide an environment where the cross-fertilisation of competences and skills are nurtured and fostered, with autonomy and responsibility restored to the individual. The goal is life-long learning, with a richer spread of knowledge, such as language and social skills, whatever profession one happens to be in.

In this chapter, we contrast different approaches to skill and training, and question the rationale behind recent policies, with reference to the human-centred approach. Vocational education is no longer either separate or inferior to the established academic mainstream. We need an alternative to the reduction of skills into elements, which can then be allegedly measured. A more human-centred approach to skill and education is one such appropriate alternative.

At the turn of the century, capital was perceived as the scarce resource and labour was seen as a commodity. In many countries developing through the industrial revolution, there was an abundance of labour, especially immigrant labour; one worker was simply interchangeable with another. Today information flows at the touch of buttons, along global digital superhighways; capital has acquired the status of a global commodity. What marks out one economy's success from others is the quantity and quality of its skilled labour. The implications are far reaching, and competitiveness hinges on effective investment in people.

The UK population has become cynical about education and training: numerous elections have been won with millions unemployed. This waste of money and resources seriously erodes the country's capacity to compete effectively with other economies, but despite this situation, the various systems for tax, benefits and grants are all geared against training and further education. Some examples illustrate this point.

- Those individuals who are in receipt of benefit may not spend in excess of 21 hours per week educating themselves, or learning new skills.
- Incentives and regional grants favour materials like buildings and equipment, rather than people investment, which is viewed as costly by companies.
- Companies are happier poaching skilled workers from other companies, rather than developing their own resources and assets. Once again we see a skills shortage, as experienced when Britain was recovering from a recession in the early 1980s.

Even at a fundamental level, young school leavers, who will form the UK labour force in coming years, cannot adequately spell or perform simple arithmetic. British skill levels, according to the Confederation of British Industry, lag up to 40% behind the world's best.

We see newly industrialised countries competing effectively against global competitors. For instance, South Korea has companies like Samsung which is now the leading manufacturer of microwave ovens; production increased from a few dozen in 1979 to over 80 000 per week in just 10 years. Unsurprisingly, the UK has proportionately fewer youngsters in further and higher education than both South Korea and Taiwan.

# Vocational vs. Academic

There is a need for more vocational training in the UK. Some psychologists argue that the pupil who assimilates on-the-job experience after starting work is more likely to excel than one who scores A grades in every subject; their talents are being wasted because educational systems only measure academic success and not practical skills. What is the appropriate balance?

Is "practical intelligence" more use than academic intelligence, and does tacit knowledge bring higher success? Professor Joel Sternberg of Yale University studied high-achieving academic students, and how their career developed in later life. His conclusions suggested that, apart from predicting university results, school grades had no correlation with later success; examination results were of no use in predicting research ability, creativity or practical abilities, although there was a weak link with analytic skills.

This study would suggest that we need to rethink academic standards and qualifications in terms of practical intelligence. After all, many entrepreneurs and captains of industry, like Alan Sugar (founder and chairman of the electronics group Amstrad) and Richard Branson (founder of the Virgin group of companies), were not grade A students.

The British government has recognised the need for policies to promote work-oriented education. Estimates from the London School of Economics (1992) suggest that two thirds of British workers have no vocational or professional qualifications, compared with only a quarter in Germany. These, and other statistics, prompted the British government to create the system of National Vocational Qualifications (NVQs) which was intended to gain parity of esteem with GCSEs and 'A' Levels.

# National Vocational Qualifications (NVQs)

In 1986 the National Council for Vocational Qualifications (NCVQ) was established, with duties to include streamlining the plethora of existing qualifications and to accredit NVQs. The council was to work closely with the three main providers of vocational courses: the Business and Technology Education Council (BTEC), the City and Guilds of London Institute and the Royal Society of Arts (RSA) Examinations Board. An ambitious target of a million holders of NVQs by 1995 was set. The council's mission was to "provide the world's most effective national framework of vocational qualifications". More recently, NVQs have also become the concern of the National Advisory Council for Education and Training Targets (NACETT). The target has been adjusted to 80% of young people to have reached NVQ level 2 (the academic equivalent of four higher-grade GCSEs; see Table 7.1) by 1997. In 1994, the realised figure was around 50%.

Britain is still some way behind Continental Europe's idea of skill training, which involves taking an examination course at college (externally assessed), combined with practical experience at work.

*Table 7.1    The five-layer NVQ framework*

| NVQ level | Equivalent to |
|---|---|
| 1 | 1-year foundation, other GCSEs |
| 2 | Basic technician; 4+ GCSEs at course grade A–C |
| 3 | Advanced technician, 2+ 'A'-levels |
| 4 | Higher technician, higher education |
| 5 | Profession, postgraduate |

# THE NEED FOR NVQS

The government had recognised the need for a vocational training scheme, as argued in White Papers in 1981 and 1986. NVQs sought to remedy several defects in the training and skilling of the workforce, including the following:

- Vocational training suffered a low status in society, with neither employers nor employees being encouraged to participate in the acquisition of skills. Hence, industry led bodies were established to formulate qualifications, all slotting into the national five-level framework. This approach, it was anticipated, would have the wholehearted support of employers, because employers should agree on skills and standards required in their sector.
- There was concern that the skills needs of UK industry were not being adequately met with existing qualifications. The emphasis was reversed from course content, duration and final examination (the input) to levels of performance required by industry (the output) assessed by practical demonstrations of competence. The application of skills, rather than the possession of skills and knowledge, is advocated.
- There was a widespread belief that restrictions to access to qualifications existed. The emphasis on formal examinations, reading, writing and numeracy skills was seen as a deterrent for many. Artificial demarcation lines, as well as age-based barriers, were highlighted for their adverse affects.

The hallmarks of the system are flexibility and transferability, with qualifications made up of a number of "units of competence"; hence individuals need never cover the same ground twice, because units should be transferable from one qualification to another.

## THE FUNDING AND COSTS

Official figures indicate that anything between three and four hundred thousand NVQs had been awarded by mid-1993.

The funding of NVQs has been interesting. Training and Enterprise Councils (TECs) have re-enforced take-up of the schemes by output-related funding initiatives. Those providers who were training on Youth Training and Employment Training schemes had 25% of their grants retained by the TECs until the individual had been awarded their NVQ (Callender 1992). This meant that trainers did not necessarily receive the full 100% funding, should the individual workers fail, and consequently internal trainers responded in a variety of ways. This approach encouraged trainers to become lax in their assessment procedures or selecting trainees for success, hence restricting opportunities to other trainees; after all, their funding was dependent on passes rather than failures. This negated the aim of NVQs, yet the funding structure increased the marginal value for companies to take-up the initiative.

Funding was only granted to trainees who gained an entire NVQ, and therefore worked against those wishing to take a variety of units from a range of NVQs encompassing a variety of different occupational areas. This was contrary to the aim of transferring skills, a principal aim of introducing NVQs.

Because of the linkage of funding with training outcomes, there was a temptation for less scrupulous agents to award qualifications to fictitious trainees. The cases that achieved publicity exposed the dangers of qualifications awarded without attendance, for the commercial gain of the agent and without proper public accountability.

Costs to the employer of introducing NVQs are reported to be high. Any medium-sized or larger employer is likely to require additional staff as trainers and assessors of the qualification. Additionally, a large amount of administrative work is created, further adding to total costs.

On a national level, the cost of implementing a competence-based approach requires extensive funding, presumably from government. Such investment can be justified only if the return is increased quality and associated benefits; we have yet to see if the anticipated benefits materialise.

## POINTS TO CONSIDER

NVQs have the potential to improve aspects of Britain's training system, but one questions whether they will ever reach the intended parity of esteem with traditional academic qualifications. The NVQ emphasis is likely to benefit the less academic, who are perhaps more motivated in a work setting, and allows individuals to obtain at least a part of a qualification, whereas before they would have nothing.

Nevertheless, the omission of written examinations in NVQs only exacerbates the problem relating to a lack of reading and writing skills, where many school leavers have basic problems with spelling; literacy and numeracy are important in modern society and in every occupation. NVQs, rather conveniently, alleviate the pressure from the education system to improve the education of school children prior to further development.

The five-level system utilised for the NVQ framework incorporates, as its lowest standard, level 1, a qualification that is significantly below European norms. This constitutes a pre-vocational standard and should perhaps be left for the school education system to cover. There is a distinct danger that NVQs will acquire a low status in the UK, which would be contrary to the initial goal; level 1 may become regarded as a test for candidates of limited ability, and certified as such as well. This trend is already visible. In continental Europe, we see great pains taken to enhance vocational schemes.

Viewed in the traditional academic sense, even level 2 is "reasonably" easy to obtain. The example of a course devised by Kirklees and Wakefield Chambers of Commerce serves to illustrate the point. A Yorkshire woman lost her factory job and spent a year unemployed. She belatedly realised that during that time she was gaining skills that would count towards a NVQ level 2 in business administration. Her experience of home budgeting, preparing letters, receiving visitors and making and receiving phone calls were used as evidence of necessary skills. The emphasis is thus on recognising and utilising the "portfolio" of skills that are perhaps not usually identified.

Table 7.2　*Distribution of NVQs by level*

| Level | Awarded | Working towards |
|-------|---------|-----------------|
| 1 | 24.4% | 26.3% |
| 2 | 59.9% | 53.4% |
| 3 | 12.9% | 14.1% |
| 4 | 2.7% | 4.5% |
| 5 | 0.1% | 1.7% |

Level 2 is by far the most popular of the five levels of NVQ, accounting for almost half of the NVQs being worked for and awarded, according to a 1993 survey published in the *Industrial Relations Review and Report* (see Table 7.2).

The approach the UK has adopted can be viewed favourably, and is presented as having the potential to give the country a world lead; however, if this is the case, have Germany, France, Sweden and other European partners all got it wrong? NVQs were emphasised as being employment-based qualifications, yet this concept is being eroded by the introduction of General National Vocational Qualifications (GNVQs), which cover broader occupational areas with correspondingly broad competencies. This is not necessarily a bad thing; the GNVQ in manufacturing, for instance, promises to develop more general competencies in engineers prior to their developing higher-level craft skills.

The dominant feature of these recent educational initiatives in the UK has been their emphasis on competence, assessed against national standards. Thus the introduction of NVQs sees a return of the Taylorist approach, in education:

the act of breaking tasks down into elements where competence is measured.

NVQs, and more recently GNVQs, are presented as challenging traditional approaches to learning and teaching. The initial issues of tacit knowledge and skill still remain unaddressed.

# The German System

In opting for the NVQ route, Britain has rejected the tested German education system twice. As long ago as 1868 the government rejected a Royal Commission's recommendation for a twin-track school system, similar to the German *Realschulen* and *Gymnasium*. Today, critics of the NVQ approach to vocational education question this judgement by the government.

August Borsig is acknowledged as the first man to build steam locomotives in Germany, yet more far-reaching was his contribution to the German education system. His creation of one of the first factory organisations, with the *meister*, or shop floor supervisor, together with the apprenticeship system, has helped to build Germany's industrial strength.

The German system is much praised, yet a study by the Institute of Economic Affairs (IEA 1992) suggests that it is a highly corporatist system, and that laws prevent people setting up handicraft workshops and other enterprises without having a *meister* qualification. German apprenticeships last three years, or more. This is seen as being too long, and it is suggested that the real purpose of the system is to prevent low-wage competition; the earnings of apprentices are only between 20% and 50% of those of their adult counterparts. In the UK, youngsters typically earn up to 85% of adult rates; this makes employers hesitate when employing the young, and reluctant to allow individuals to take time out for training.

# The Apprentice: Twentieth-century Dodo

Practical actions are most commonly associated with traditional crafting skills; blowing glass to make something usable and beautiful is an extremely difficult skill for the uninitiated, and the act evokes a feeling of awe. Skills like glass blowing, furniture making, erecting a stone wall, throwing a pot and so on require years of practice in order to become a master. The long years required to acquire these skills are discouraging.

Traditionally, apprenticeships were commonplace; is this still the case? Certainly, in the UK, the role and status of the apprentice has changed and evolved dramatically during the last three decades, yet German counterparts have managed to retain their system while still evolving and improving it. The supposed differences from the German system were not that stark a few decades ago. The UK system in operation during the 1960s, when Industrial Training Boards (ITBs) were established, had some similarities to the German one.

In an initiative to establish a vocational training system, national standards were set by industry-based ITBs, with qualifications awarded being industry-based and, importantly, supported by further education. Costs were shared by employers through a compulsory payment scheme, so as to discourage poaching from other organisations. A levy grant system ensured that all contributed, and that those who trained in sufficient numbers (and sufficiently well) were reimbursed. This approach, although with less external control, is similar to the German system in existence today. The principles retain the support of employers and trades unions in the UK, but not, at present, of government.

Apprenticeship schemes existed and flourished, some derived from the pre-industrial-revolution guilds, involving agreements between unions, employers and young employees. Typically, the length of time served in a scheme was some five years, much as in Germany, where partners co-operate in vocational training based on formal apprenticeships, complemented by further education.

In that past age, companies viewed good training schemes as an essential ingredient for recruitment, manpower planning and emancipatory development; training was not then subject to the short-termism of government policies and, or, accounting pressures. Engineering training centres were established with the Engineering Industry Training Board (EITB).

During the 1970s and 1980s, the UK experienced dramatic periods of recession and during these depressionary periods, training was one of the first victims. Companies did not want to train beyond their immediate needs, and unions managed to secure high wage rates for those without vocational qualifications, making training expensive. Furthermore, training was too long at five years, even though this had been cut down from seven years.

Germany experienced these problems as well as the UK, but the German reaction was very different. The Germans considered the time spent to be still essential for effective training, and cut the number of years required from five to three; the system was enforced in every employment area. They improved their system to make it work better. In the UK, the system changed in a rather *ad hoc* manner. Initiatives launched in the recessionary periods were focused on keeping large numbers occupied, rather than on a high quality of training; the decline of quality training in industry was left to continue.

The late 1980s saw the introduction of the National Council for Vocational Qualifications, whose role was similar to the German *Bundesinstitut für Berufsbildung* (Federal Institute for Vocational Training).

Today, as ever, there is a continued need for an effective and rewarding apprenticeship system, in order to maintain an adequate UK craft skills base. Despite the continual industrial problems in Britain, the traditional concept of the apprentice still remains loosely intact, but questions about the new vocational initiative are still unanswered. What effect will the decomposition of traditional skills into measurable units have on the teaching and training of skills?

# Manufacturing in Britain

*"Thatcher cleared the undergrowth. The problem is she forgot to plant a few trees."*

*Mark Radcliffe, CBI National Manufacturing Council*

The UK manufacturing base has been weakened by years of neglect, and a decade of industrial euthanasia. In 1993 British manufacturing productivity was 40% lower than America and Germany, 30% lower than Japan and 25% lower than France. Only 2% of British factories are deemed to be of world class.

Manufacturing is vital to the UK economy. Although it comprises only 20% of the total, it forms 50% of consumer spending and 70% of exports.

A career in manufacturing has come to be viewed with less status than its business-oriented counterparts. In many countries there is growing concern that young people are rejecting industry as a career, because it is perceived to be hierarchical and authoritarian. Figure 7.1 shows that the proportion of technical graduates entering industry in the UK has declined, and evidence has shown that this will continue. Manufacturing is only one of many sectors that need to pay greater attention to the working environment to reverse this trend. Human-centred systems can, to some extent, provide a framework in which industry can be a more attractive and rewarding career choice. Emancipatory development follows from the use of creative human abilities and good supporting information systems.

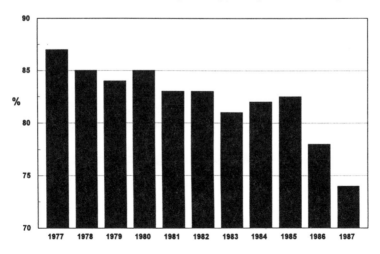

*Figure 7.1    Engineering graduates entering industry. Source: PA Consulting*

## THE ROLE OF SCIENCE

'A'-level examination results in British schools have been indicating for some time that a diminishing number of students want to study science. In the UK there have been moves to convert would-be art students into scientists by offering attractive grants. It is not surprising that students opt for other subjects, as they are often less demanding and, importantly, are more materially rewarding. Young researchers today suffer from insecure and inadequately funded projects.

Science is important, not only to profits and economic performance, but also to culture, health and better management and understanding of the world we live in. Most established scientists credit the inspiration and aspirations that set them on their course to talented teachers. Arguably the teachers are still as professional and talented: what has changed?

William Waldegrave's White Paper on the organisation of science (*Realising Our Potential*) offered much, but managed to deliver very little. The first White Paper on science and technology for 21 years was modest in its rhetoric. Following cabinet reshuffles even the rhetoric was reduced.

For decades there has been a paradoxical situation where Britain has excelled in science, its immense national asset, but has still been hounded by rather lacklustre economic performance. The main points of the White Paper, which proposed to harness Britain's strength in science and technology, are outlined below:

- The large Science and Engineering Research Council was to be split, hence retaining the dual funding system by the universities and research councils. A new Council for Science was established. The system of allowing scientific decisions to be made through research councils, initially established by Lord Haldane in 1918, still lives in principle. The Advisory Council on Science and Technology was abolished.
- The traditional PhD was no longer considered as ideal training, with more emphasis placed on Masters courses. Graduates wanting to pursue a higher degree are now expected to undertake a one-year MSc course, and funding for PhD positions has been reduced.
- 'Technology foresight', a new technique, was developed in order to identify key areas for investment, with each sector of technology examined by panels of experts.
- Despite pressure to increase funding, no additional resources were allocated.

This White Paper promised to begin the process of ending the sclerosis of British science. For too long, science has been subordinate to the arts and this is reflected in public policy as well; this is not surprising, because most politicians originate from an arts-related education. We finally see a minister to represent science at government level, but is this just paying lip-service to the problem?

The Office of Science and Technology is only responsible for a sixth of government backed research, and its relationship with the DTI, which is responsible for technology, is muddy at best. In contrast, the White Paper makes the relationship with the Ministry of Defence quite clear. There were no proposals for the conversion from defence to civil research, even though we have seen the end of the cold war, and the fact that the Ministry of Defence is responsible for 40% of public R&D funds.

Britain has an excellent record of discoveries, inversely related to the capital spent on research and development, yet industry is unable to exploit the potential results. The old syndrome of "not invented here" is still far too prevalent in British thinking. How many are aware of the numerous British Nobel prize winners? How many can actually name them? Why is there no Nobel prize for manufacturing?

# What is Management Training?

This question poses some difficult and awkward issues, and the initial response may be given in terms of academic abstractions coupled with identified vocational skills. Further thinking on the subject may further evolve the answer into Tayloristic discrete attributes and identifiable competences – a solution of limited use that does not capture the richness of education. What you can be sure of is that each answer will be different.

Only the English language has the word "manage"; when used colloquially, it has a meaning which has little to do with the formal definition. "How did you manage to solve that problem?" There is a feeling of ingenuity and improvisation, rather than planning and organisation. How can this be taught? Does one have to learn by experience and reflection?

## THE FUTURE OF MANAGEMENT TRAINING

In 1988, a meeting backed by the British Institute of Management and the Confederation of British Industry spawned the Management Charter Initiative (MCI). The MCI had at its core a belief in the importance of competent management; the non-profit-making organisation has more than 1300 members from the private, public and voluntary sectors. The purpose of the organisation was not to carry out training, but to encourage the correct conditions for managers to take advantage of training opportunities.

Studies (Handy 1987) had already indicated that Britain possessed one of the lowest levels of professional trained managers, with only 10% having professional training. This was certainly not the case in other developed countries. When looking at academic qualifications (Table 7.3) the results are equally startling. The figures for directors in Germany are even more contrasting, with 54% of the management board holding doctorate degrees – not in management but typically in science, engineering or law. The first MCI study confirmed what many had suspected all along, and certainly corroborated the Handy study conducted a year earlier.

- One fifth of the largest UK companies had carried out no management training in the previous 12 months.
- One in three managers had had no training since starting work.
- Four out of five managers had no degree or professional qualification.

Table 7.3   Academic qualifications

| Degree attainment | % holding a degree |
|---|---|
| British managers | 24 |
| Japanese managers | 85 |
| US managers | 85 |

The challenge for MCI has been to stress the link between management development and profit; in the UK, it is financial results that provide the initial impetus for management development.

Better, more able managers who are capable of thinking and working across traditional functional boundaries are essential for today's corporate business environment. We see less layers of management, with the pyramid becoming ever flatter. This places great emphasis on managers to be able to work in different roles with varying responsibilities. The managers of tomorrow will not be those who have mastered only one discipline as a passport to a lifetime career, and refuse to expand their knowledge, beliefs and experience.

## THE MBA

Companies that have realised the benefits of improved management education are increasingly funding and encouraging their employees to obtain a Master of Business Administration (MBA) qualification. This in turn has created an impetus for providers of management development programmes, including the MBA.

Much of industry has questioned the ability of management training providers, usually university business schools, to keep up with the needs of companies. One opinion, by the Economic Intelligence Unit (EIU 1992), suggests that "many organisations express irritability with management development specialists, especially the business schools". The report praises the UK business schools for having better developed strategies on partnerships with their clients than most counterparts on the continent and in the USA.

How does an individual who is interested in obtaining an MBA choose between the plethora of business schools offering the qualification, especially since the early 1980s? How can one determine the "quality" of the education and training provided? Each MBA, at each business school, demands a different fee. Should the price reflect the quality? Can we assume that you get what you pay for? Certain standards exist, but these are far from robust.

In the UK, the Association of MBAs (AMBA) polices the institutions offering the qualification, and has only accredited about a third of suppliers. Furthermore there is no requirement for accreditation before anyone can offer a course and call it an MBA.

Continental European counterparts are somewhat different. In France, management training is the domain of *Grandes Écoles*, not universities, with more demanding admission standards. They are long established, many over a hundred years' old, and academic standards are high. Indeed, many experts in the field argue that France's INSEAD business school is the best in the world.

France is strict in its accreditation; *Grandes Écoles* are governed by the *Fondation Nationale pour l'Enseignement et la Gestion des Enterprises* (FNEGE), and are ranked in strict order. In the USA there is the American Association of Collegiate Schools of Business (AACSB), and affiliation is a guarantee that the school's qualifications are of a high standard.

The ages of average students differ. The MBA, a US import, was designed for people who have at least two years' experience in business before they start the course. This means that in the UK the average MBA graduate is between 28 and 30 years of age. In Germany the age is even higher, where work experience is a more highly valued requirement. This is not the case in France, where it is normal for a 23-year-old to have an MBA.

The choice of which MBA, at which institution, is a difficult one, but it is important to understand that one is not inherently better than the other; they are just different. There will always be a role for different type of courses, but some element of standard is needed to counter comparisons between MBAs. The NCVQ has, through its agent the MCI, begun to impose uniform standards on management courses qualifying for NVQ status at various levels, corresponding to certificate, diploma and masters.

# Management Training and a Competence Approach

1992 saw the launch of the Institute of Management (IM), bringing together the former British Institute of Management and the Institute of Industrial Managers; it is claimed to be Europe's largest management institute, and its primary aim is to raise the profile of management training, with emphasis on developing management competences.

Individuals heading the organisation are centred on advocating a competence approach to management training. The IM provides "competent manager" programmes, comprising self-study packages leading to a certificate and diploma in management at NVQ levels 4 and 5. The competence approach is consistent with recent government changes to the education system, and it cannot be asserted that management training is only academic; there are other facets to effective management training: skill, knowledge and self-development. Perhaps the learning of the *ability* to learn is the most important factor. Established universities are developing programmes that satisfy the requirements both of knowledge and of competence.

# Quality

# 8

Decades ago, the quality of a company's goods and services provided differentiation from others in the market, especially in mass-production industries. Organisations benefited from this approach, and used it to compete against other companies in the world market, but this condition no longer holds true; high quality is now a pre-condition of world competitiveness.

In Europe, modern quality concepts are developing strongly towards a synthesis of concepts of quality that are deeply rooted in the social and cultural diversity of European traditions. These traditions and cultures that are shaping the quality movement in Europe share the same ancestral roots as human-centred systems. In the short term, Europe is still in the quest for excellence, but there is a danger that attempts to transplant the Japanese and US systems of quality into a different cultural base could endanger the viability of industrial competitiveness in the long term.

Like Deming's precepts on quality, human-centred systems are concerned with people and working practices; they share similar goals and principles. European competitiveness is embracing what can be termed the softer side of quality (management, skills, culture and working life, as well as the social aspects of the quality movement), i.e. more than just statistical methods of reducing waste, which is only one dimension of quality.

Europe has approached the quality issue later than some of its industrial competitors, but it has garnered a different, more tacitly human-centred approach, which builds on its cultural strengths. Other countries are learning and adapting their own practices from the experience of these approaches. This chapter explores these strengths, and how they fit into the human-centred framework; it also sheds light on areas of concern.

# The Search for Total Quality

One of the most enduring concepts in the theory of management in the business and industrial sector, and more recently in the public, voluntary, and academic sectors, is the elusive total quality management (TQM). Quality has become akin to the emperor's new clothes in the well-known fairy story; quality has the role of the new clothes – top people want it, you are supposed to feel better for wearing it, but nobody is quite sure what it is!

The origins of the movement can be traced back to Walter Shewhart, a business executive who in the 1920s devised a method of using statistics to control the quality of telephones manufactured at the AT&T Hawthorne works in Chicago. Employees at the plant included W. Edward Deming and Joseph Juran, who became disciples of Shewhart's methods. These two individuals, together with others, notably Philip Crosby and Armand Feigenbaum, can be acknowledged as the founding fathers of the quality movement. The theories of these individuals, which the Japanese took to heart, have helped to create the industrial goliath that Japanese postwar industry has become. Deming's work in turn was highly influenced by the work of Japanese statisticians and engineers, like the founder of the Japanese Union of Scientists and Engineers (JUSE).

It was not until the late 1970s that the industrial West belatedly began to embrace the concepts that have helped the Japanese establish quality as the entry point to whole industries. The quality movement has now permeated the majority of our corporations and institutions, and is one element of greater transformation. TQM remains better understood and more widely accepted in North America (where arguably it was invented) and in Japan (where it was first properly applied). Europe has finally begun the process of embracing quality as a fundamental business practice in the past two decades.

# What is TQM?

At its barest, TQM is the process of applying quality throughout an organisation, with the goal of improving all of its processes, customers and products or services; it is the quest for competitive advantage. The British Standards Institution (BSI) defines total quality management as (British Standards Institution 1991):

> *"A management philosophy embracing all activities through which the needs and expectations of the customer and the community, and the objectives of the organisation, are satisfied in the most efficient and cost-effective way by maximising the potential of all employees in a continuing drive for improvement."*

Research indicates that companies can spend up to 25 to 30% of their operating budgets rectifying errors in their production (and other) processes, while estimates further suggest that a third of an organisation's effort is spent dealing with errors and checks (Oakland 1989). Exponents of TQM claim, on the other hand, that up to half these costs can be saved by getting things right the first time round.

The example of a Japanese electronics company illustrates the point. Hiroshi Hamada, president of Ricoh, quotes the cost of correcting a fault in a photocopier the firm produces as; $368 at the design stage, $17 000 before shipment and $590 000 when it is with the customer. The recent fault in Pentium microprocessors, involving Intel in costs of some $500 million in replacing all products already sold, further illustrates the point.

Applying quality techniques, such as TQM or some element of it, is not the instant medicine for low productivity and declining profits. The quality movement has been in existence for decades, but as with all great approaches, the implementation often disintegrates into petty techniques. The problem is exacerbated in latter day economies by the many quality "consultants" who are akin to the miraculous snake oil medicine men of early day America; today they are industrial patent medicine men promising organisations instant liberation from economic malaise.

Quality is not just a public relations exercise, as it is sometimes viewed, and requires a transformation of the philosophy of an organisation, the extent of which is often underestimated.

# Benchmarking

"If you know your enemy and know yourself, you need not fear the results of a hundred battles."

*Sun Tzu, 500 BC*

Self-knowledge is the key. A strategic management tool that has already proved its worth, and grows increasingly more popular, is benchmarking, which can be defined as: "The continuous measuring of a company's services and processes against those of its toughest competitors, or world class organisations" (Camp 1989). Up to 80% of the Fortune 500 companies are estimated to use benchmarking in some form. The tool is increasingly being associated with TQM and BPR techniques.

Xerox was one of the first organisations to use benchmarking, as understood in its contemporary sense. In attempting to retain its dominance in the copier market, with increasing threats from Far Eastern companies, the organisation introduced a series of benchmarking studies to determine the scope of the competition. Of course, the origins of benchmarking go back much further, as the above passage from an ancient Chinese general, Sun Tzu, illustrates. Camp (Camp 1989) quotes Sun Tzu, and offers a useful working definition of benchmarking as: "the search for best industry practices that will lead to superior performance".

Benchmarking is not restricted to the manufacturing sector, or to direct competitors. Other organisations in the same sector are a useful starting point, and competitors are an obvious focus for comparison, but the most useful information is often qualitative rather than quantitative, and non-competitors are often willing to share experiences on how tasks are performed.

Critics of benchmarking highlight the difficulties in obtaining information on competitors and/or competing projects, and claim the practice is in the same league as industrial espionage. Much is dependant on how the application is utilised; used solely in emulating, the advantages would be short-lived anyway. While the act of benchmarking is legal, users of the technique need to work within an ethical framework where information is not gathered illegally, and information on proprietary products and processes should not be obtained. The dividing line between benchmarking and industrial espionage can be a fine one.

Many service organisations now provide facilities for benchmarking, either in isolation or as part of a larger programme of change. Arthur Andersen, the accountancy firm with a large consultancy arm, invested $10 million in producing its proprietary Global Best Practices Knowledge Base, based on Andersen's surveys in various industries. A. T. Kearney, a consultancy company, provides services centred on its Best-Of-Best benchmarking survey. Within the BESTMAN project, the BESTMAN questionnaire tool was devised to facilitate the benchmarking of an organisation on the BESTMAN generic model (see Appendix 4).

Recent years have seen the establishment of clearing houses to share benchmarking information, including the International Benchmark Clearing House and the Strategic Planning Institute Council on Benchmarking, a nonprofit organisation.

As well as BESTMAN, other collaborative projects are also embracing benchmarking techniques. The Inter-Company Productivity Group (ICPG), an informal club of 16 large multinationals, covers a broad range of issues as well as benchmarking and quality (including BPR, organisation structure, innovation, IT, education and so on). Its members include British Airways, Courtaulds, Unilever and the UK operations of Nissan, Heinz and 3M.

In a global marketplace it can be difficult for companies to identify their competitors. There is a critical need, by companies and those concerned with strategies for economic development, for better awareness of the competitor environment, especially in the UK, where managers and executives are branded myopic and complacent. This is evident even in the ICPG, where a consultant for the group carried out an opinion and benchmarking survey in 1993. Senior managers who were surveyed displayed little knowledge of their competitor's performance in 17 highlighted areas that were deemed to be critical to success. Benchmarking provides an invaluable base to build upon when attempts are made to rectify situations like these.

# The Quality Standards

Many standards for measuring quality have been established over time, some of which are now internationally recognised as a measure of attaining "quality procedures". These provide an essential and needy framework for business in all sectors. Two sets of standards in particular have recently gained prominence, and are now discussed below.

## BS 5750 (ISO 9000 and EN 29000)

The British Standards Institution (BSI), founded as the Engineering Standards Association in 1901, launched BS 5750 in the UK in 1979 to improve the quality of British management, and it has since become an internationally recognised standard. What started life as a UK Ministry of Defence code for ensuring value for money on large purchases has now been taken up in Europe as EN 29000 and round the world as ISO 9000. The international variants are gaining in significance.

BS 5750 has become a victim of its own success, and has been taken up by many large companies, who are well equipped to handle the large volumes of paperwork that are required. Recently, other organisations have adopted the standard, either by choice or because they have been obliged to by market forces. Organisations such as accountants, chambers of commerce, educational institutions and even a prison (Holloway, in the UK) are dedicated to continuous improvement.

However much the standard has grown in popularity, with over 22 000 businesses having registered, its image has now been tarnished and it now has the reputation of being expensive and inappropriate. This is especially the case for SMEs, which now face the paradoxical and extremely difficult situation where companies in every sector are beginning to insist on buying only from companies that have succeeded in obtaining the standard. The example of Marks & Spencer (M&S), the retailing giant, illustrates this situation: many of its suppliers are required to have obtained BS 5750, yet M&S declines to register for the standard itself. M&S does not need BS 5750 in order to gain quality image, but it uses BS 5750 as a discipline for potential suppliers, a hurdle to be cleared.

### Problems with Quality Procedures

Unlike most British Standards, BS 5750 is a measure of quality *procedures* and hence open to individual interpretation; it does not govern the quality of the goods or service produced; indeed, BSI advocates reporting any firm who claims its product meets BS 5750 to trading standards officers under the Trade Descriptions Act. One might therefore question the intrinsic worth of achieving certification, especially when this can cost £5000 for only a small business.

Quoting BSI material, the standard provides "...assurance that an organisation is following its own procedure to ensure the quality of its products or services", so that a company offering a callout service within 10 days, for example, as opposed to its competitor's 24 hours, can still comply with the standard, as long as consistency is maintained.

Despite the standard's widespread adoption, a number of factors have blemished its status:

- The standard gained much popularity when in 1988 the Department of Trade and Industry (DTI) agreed to pay from 50 to 66% of the consultancy costs (up to £1200 per day) incurred by companies registering for the standard. What has now become a marketing tool was in fact subsidised by the taxpayer until late 1993.
- Surprisingly, a standard BS 5750 certification form does not exist! The DTI established the National Accreditation Council for Certification Bodies (NACCB), of which the BSI is a member, together with 31 other purely commercial organisations, for the purpose of adjudicating and awarding certificates. Non-accredited organisations may also award certificates, however; so anyone can set themself up as a consultant, and subsequently as an assessor advising companies on the standard, regardless of the "quality" of the advice given.
- The standard generates large quantities of paperwork because of the need to formalise procedures. The example of Wessex Water illustrates the point; when registering for BS 5750, the documentation of the company's quality systems exceeded 22 000 pages, encompassed in 164 manuals.
- Usually, no indication is given about which range of activities the standard has been obtained for: a small division employing a few people, or the entire organisation? Companies are not legally obliged to be precise.
- The emphasis within the standard is on processes, and the quality standard's origins lie in the manufacturing industry. The applicability of BS 5750 to the service industries is questionable.

With many issues unresolved, both the quality of the standard itself and the means of obtaining it are in question. Would the BSI pass its own quality management standard? What does holding the standard imply about the quality of management and managers?

## THE ENVIRONMENTAL STANDARD: BS 7750

With increasing concerns about environmental issues, the BSI has developed the cousin of BS 5750, with many of the same problems. Both share the same theme: compliance with BS 5750 is no guarantee of an organisation's output being of high quality, as low targets can be set; similarly, compliance with BS 7750 does not necessarily ensure good environmental performance. The BSI seems to have rushed a standard in order to prepare itself for participation in the EU's eco-management and audit scheme (EMAS), in full operation from 1995.

Other countries' equivalents also have their own problems in this relatively new area. For example:

- The USA has legislative environmental law in place, and companies typically spend large amounts of money employing lawyers to ensure that minimum standards are being met. In situations of dispute, it is the lawyers who gain once again. Even the US Super Fund, established by common consent to deal with large-scale environmental damage, has re-directed more revenue into lawyers' pockets than into environmental protection.
- The high standards Germany set were applauded by environmentalists, but smothering regulation is now distorting the picture. The government has found it necessary to bail out its regulatory body, at huge cost, with many regions in rebellion against new laws on recycling all packaging; it now costs individual companies more than it is worth – as least in the short term – to dispose of waste, although it is difficult to place a value on the wider social aspects of the policy.

Both EMAS and BS 7750 are voluntary schemes, but they represent different implementations and interpretations. EMAS requires an environmental review of the organisation, followed by an improvement programme and backed by a published statement, which is verified by an expert in the field. Both the environmental impact of the company's work and the programme to mitigate it are detailed, and it will initially be applied only to industrial sites. In contrast, BS 7750 is intended to apply to any and every business and institution. It could fail in the same area as the one where BS 5750 has received so much criticism; local authorities, as well as other organisations, would use the stipulations of the standard as criteria for awarding orders, thus placing increasing burdens on smaller businesses.

# The Quality Awards

Many quality-awarding authorities have been established world-wide over the years. They all share a common theme: rewarding organisations for achieving quality-related excellence. It seems that the existence of quality awards does improve quality consciousness in business around the world, but does it really pay to participate and win? What are the associated costs of attempting to be a victor in the national and international quality competitions?

Research has indicated that the existence of these awards has inspired and motivated organisations to place quality foremost, to their own subsequent advantage. This is not exclusively the case, however. Florida Power & Light, the first non-Japanese company to win the Deming Prize (discussed below) found itself in serious trouble almost immediately after winning. It had become obsessed with applying itself to the quality principles required to win the prize, at the expense of other factors. Arguably, it was a case of "never mind about the customer, just feel the quality".

The more established and well-known quality awards share some common principles, but are different in their underlying philosophy and maturity. They can be placed into two broad categories:

- Non-prescriptive awards, where scoring criteria or examples of past winning attributes are deliberately not detailed. Examples of this group include:
  - The Deming Prize
  - The British Quality Award

- The second group provide the criteria to be used as a basis of self-assessment; full details of awarding criteria are disseminated, whether or not the organisation wishes to compete for the award. Examples include:
  - The Malcolm Baldrige Award
  - European Quality Award
  - The Presidential Award for Quality

## THE DEMING AWARD

Deming, during his first visit to Japan, impressed businessmen with the importance of statistical quality control to such an extent that the Deming Prize was created in 1951 by the Japanese Union of Scientists and Engineers (JUSE). It was awarded to companies that had shown impressive quality advances in a variety of highlighted areas, and is the world's oldest, and perhaps most prestigious, quality award. A synopsis of the checklist is provided in Table 8.1 (Ishikawa 1985).

Table 8.1   The Deming Award checklist criteria

|   | Deming Prize Checklist |
|---|---|
| 1 | Policy and objectives |
| 2 | Organisation and its operation |
| 3 | Education and its dissemination |
| 4 | Assembling and disseminating information and its utilisation |
| 5 | Analysis |
| 6 | Standardisation |
| 7 | Control |
| 8 | Quality assurance |
| 9 | Effects |
| 10 | Future plans |

The checklist has no maximum scores attributed to each category, and assessors have the freedom to interpret each case on its own merits; in this it differs from its European and American counterparts.

In 1969, in commemoration of the first International Conference on Quality Control in Tokyo, the Japan Quality Control Award was created. The award is presented to organisations that have won the Deming Prize in more than five previous years, and ensures that companies that have won the Deming Prize do not become slack and complacent in their efforts towards continuous improvement.

The Deming Prize has been a significant catalyst in improving the quality of goods produced by Japanese firms. At the time of its birth, Japanese products were often viewed in the West as little better than junk: tinny plastic radios and poorly constructed gadgets. Today manufactured goods bearing names such as Nikon, Sony and Toyota are likened in quality terms to the Swiss watches and Hasselblad cameras of an earlier era.

The Prize has also contributed significantly to the stability of companies, with none of the prizewinners going out of business. When examining key performance indicators, prize winners are ahead of the rest again. Over a period of 20 years, from 1969 to 1989, the profits of prizewinners increased to an average of 14%, while Japanese industry in general managed 12% compared with US industry's 7%. Profit margins in prizewinning companies were also significantly higher during this period (Chew 1989). The prize, named after perhaps the best-known American in Japan, has only once been won by a non-Japanese company: the American Florida Power & Light organisation, which won it in 1989.

# THE MALCOLM BALDRIGE NATIONAL QUALITY AWARD

The USA followed the Japanese example, albeit 36 years later, with the Malcolm Baldrige Award, named after a US Commerce Secretary. The origins can be attributed to the fear of the Japanese industrial machine and the need to compete. This is ironic, as modern quality theories originated in the USA.

The award is given to companies that have excelled at achieving TQM, and the winners are expected to share and diffuse their knowledge and experiences with other businesses. Each year, the award is ceremonially presented by the US president to a maximum of six companies. Judges seek adherence to a set of underlying tenets of quality, especially the belief that the customer is the important judge of a company's quality. Companies should also be seen to build relationships with firms outside their own organisations, such as suppliers and the local community. Seven categories are utilised, as outlined in Table 8.2.

The important aspect of the award is to promote quality awareness throughout American businesses, and it is subsequently geared towards providing a means of self-assessment. Figures for submissions for the competition have remained relatively static over the past five years, whereas the applications for the detailed guidelines have escalated by a factor of 25, of which only one in 3000 copies distributed elicits a formal application (Brockman 1993).

*Table 8.2   The Baldrige Award checklist criteria*

| | Baldrige Award checklist | Points |
|---|---|---|
| 1 | Management of process quality | 140 |
| 2 | Senior executive leadership | 90 |
| 3 | Human resource development and management | 150 |
| 4 | Strategic quality planning | 60 |
| 5 | Information and analysis | 80 |
| 6 | Customer focus and satisfaction | 300 |
| 7 | Quality and operational results | 180 |

Apostles of the award, such as Robert Galvin, the chairman of Motorola, call it "the most important catalyst for transforming American business". Despite this praise and much more like it from other major corporations, the Baldrige award has attracted its critics, who suggest that it is flawed in many areas including methodology, focus and philosophy. The latter point is a crucial one. The Baldrige award lacks a coherent and strong philosophy, unlike the Deming Prize, which is based on the ideas of Deming, himself a strong critic of the Baldridge Award, and indeed the criteria laid down by the governing organisation, the National Institute of Standards and Technology, are very broad.

The largest flaw in the award is the fact that there are only a limited number of winners; it is effectively a competition between firms. Surely this inhibits co-operation between organisations, one of the principal factors that the Baldrige Award was established to achieve.

## EUROPEAN FOUNDATION FOR QUALITY MANAGEMENT

Major European companies established the European Foundation for Quality Management (EFQM) in 1988 to improve the position of European industry in world markets, and conceived a yearly award, to be presented to companies exhibiting quality excellence. The criteria utilised to evaluate potential winners of the EQFM are outlined in Table 8.3. As with the Baldrige Award, a maximum number of total points are allocated in each category and a detailed explanation of the criteria is freely available to encourage self-assessment.

*Table 8.3   The EQFM Award checklist criteria*

| | EQFM Award checklist | Points |
|---|---|---|
| 1 | Leadership | 100 |
| 2 | People management | 90 |
| 3 | Policy and strategy | 80 |
| 4 | Processes | 140 |
| 5 | Customer satisfaction | 200 |
| 6 | Business results | 150 |
| 7 | Impact on society | 60 |
| 8 | Resources | 90 |
| 9 | People satisfaction | 90 |

Recent winners of the award present an embarrassing quandary for the Foundation: in 1993 the European operations of the textile group Milliken took first prize and the manufacturing and supplies division of ICL came second, followed by Rank Xerox in third place. The startling point is that all of the victors are foreign-owned: Milliken is a US company, based in Georgia, ICL is an 80% subsidiary of Fujitsu of Japan and Rank Xerox is 50% controlled by the US Xerox Corporation. This situation reinforces the opinion that quality is a better understood and applied process in Japan and the US. Quality is more than just a matter of presentation.

# TQM in the Public Sector: An Oxymoron?

Increasingly, we see the quality management movement extending into the public sector. Fundamental to the quality approach is attending to the wishes of the customer, which are as important in the public sector as in the private sector. This extension has far-reaching consequences for the society we live in, and has already had startling impacts.

## EDUCATION

What does quality status in an educational institution entail? Certainly, many colleges and universities have been successful in achieving BS 5750, covering quality assurance in procedures, but quality education is more than just conformance to documented procedures.

Education has long been subject to quality checks on teaching and learning by Her Majesty's Inspectors (HMI), who have been concerned with standards on a national level. Yet HMI have been reluctant to quantify their verdicts, and school governing bodies are now entitled to commission their own inspections. The applicability of the BS 5750 model to the service sector is also further questioned by the manner in which "quality" is attributed to educational institutions. Cooley (Cooley 1987) states that: "Our UK universities can be likened to being organised as factories, with students referred to as commodities, examinations as quality control procedures, professors as operators and graduation as delivery."

The factory model of schooling has in fact dominated American education, and ironically it is this model that has been imposed on British schools via the 1988 Education Act. This has displaced a more humanistic treatment that was evolving in many schools, not unlike the Deming approach, which is morally relevant to education.

## HEALTH

The effects of TQM on the health of Americans has been startling. In a country that spends almost 15% of its gross national product (GNP) on an insurance-based health-care system, TQM only comes below cost cutting and containment. So far, most of the initiatives have centred on improving the bureaucratic administrative process, but of more concern is the notion of quality in medicine. Engineering projects built with defects can be reworked, and the component, or product, in question can still be of worthwhile use. The question of patients who are treated wrongly, who may suffer unnecessarily or not recover at all, poses a far more controversial issue. Is it ethical *not* to have quality techniques in health?

Managers in a hospital in Kansas City claim that they have cut the number of deaths in the hospital by 20% after introducing a total-quality programme. Small specialist teams monitored accidents, including patient deaths, and presented the results to physicians and ward teams. Consequently, clinical and administrative policies were changed (*Financial Times* 6 March 1992). Such stories from the USA have lessons for the UK, especially as the National Health Service Management Executive has invested over £2.5 million since 1990 in supporting TQM initiatives. There are problems in applying concepts of quality to health care; is quality to be measured by compliance to agreed set procedures, or by the condition and well-being of the patient on discharge?

In welfare, the idea of quality for the consumer has a different perspective and emphasis than in the private sector. When making a purchase, a consumer is seeking to obtain an item that is better than any equivalent unit produced by any other manufacturer or retailer. In the private sector, consumerism advocates obtaining the "best buy". According to the simple market-forces model, if others do not get this or its equivalent, then it does not really matter. In contrast, improved health services usually relate to getting something that is better than before, rather than better than others. People do not want a service that is better than others, but simply one that is as good as possible.

One of the most promising aspects of TQM is the encouragement of the empowerment of staff, who should have the required skills to take responsibility. The potential emancipatory development could begin to help reverse the trend of valued staff being lured to other sectors. Quality in health care is more elusive than it is in other sectors, and at its best can save lives. At its least, more medical records could be found, and telephones answered more quickly – gains that should not be dismissed lightly.

# The Quality of Life

The huge emphasis on quality is justified, but what seems to have been forgotten, or ignored, is the quality of working life. Most of the industrialised world is now realising that the problem is not a lack of *having*, but a lack of *being*. There is a need for an anti-Taylorist reorganisation of work; Taylor's views of the worker did not include the intrinsic motivation of the individual and the general needs of humans, but utilised money and goals as forms of extrinsic reinforcement (workers were rewarded beyond an established standard of performance).

Finally, we see society today beginning to move towards an organisation of work that focuses on leisure rather than on consumption. The EU Social Chapter proposes a cut in working hours. In France, a reduction from 39 to 35 hours a week would create a million extra jobs over five years.

We begin to see the antithesis of the "greed is good" paradigm, epitomised by Oliver Stone's fictional character, Gordon Gekko, which was rampant in the 1980s. Gekko, a highly successful player on the Wall Street markets, made millions of dollars from manipulating whole organisations with financial muscle, and reaped the benefits from the results.

Increasing attention is being paid by corporations and government to the environment and the ethical framework that we live and work in, but the need for flexibility by organisations continues to drive the normal nine-to-five working schedule into obscurity. When we examined working trends in the past 20 years, we can clearly see the working week being increased in hourly terms, typically embracing late-night periods and weekends. The concept of overtime may disappear in another decade should the trend continue.

The benefits of increased productivity have too often been taken in monetary terms, by working longer hours, rather than leisure time; average incomes have almost doubled in the past two decades in the industrialised countries. This has not been without cost: the richest 10% of society has benefited, with the poorest 10% actually becoming poorer in real terms. There is increasing concern today over the distribution of wealth.

## THE "KAROSHI" SYNDROME

Our Japanese counterparts, who have lived with their system of neo-feudal corporatism, are beginning to realise that their quality of life is depressingly poor, despite the fact that Japan enjoys one of the highest per-capita incomes in the world. Sararimen (white-collar workers) are leaving work, at 6 p.m. instead of 10 p.m., to return to their horrendously expensive tiny flats, two-thirds of which are not even connected to the main sewers. In the Japanese manufacturing industries, so admired in the Western hemisphere, workers are often working at weekends and late into the night. Group pressure ensures that workers follow the leads of their colleagues. The situation is at its worst in the SME sector, where 50-to 60-hour working weeks are the norm.

In fact, the Japanese work from 200 to 250 hours a year more than their US and European counterparts, and this does not even include overtime. One survey, in the *Mainichi Daily News* in 1989, concludes that the annual working hours including overtime for a Japanese worker are 2159, compared with 1546 hours for a German worker.

Tokyo, at 1992 prices, is reported to be worth more than all the real estate of the United States put together, with the site of the Imperial palace considered more valuable than Canada, the second largest country in the world (Alexander 1992).

Working and living in these environments has had its stress-related repercussions: the deeply rooted Japanese work ethos has led to about 2000 Japanese literally working themselves to death per year, a syndrome known as *karoshi* (already mentioned in Chapter 2). *Karoshi*, meaning "sudden death from overwork", hardly squares with the Japanese ethos of the workplace being an environment where fulfilment, self-actualisation and enlightenment can be discovered. Although *karoshi* hit mostly blue-collar workers about 10 years ago, it now affects all types of workers in a variety of different occupations and is reported to affect up to 10 000 Japanese workers annually.

Further examination of the phenomenon indicates that *karoshi* is more than just working too hard. We all know of a colleague or friend who may work extremely long hours, whether as a busy executive or perhaps a farmer tending his land and working from dawn till dark, yet they do not actually *die* from their work. After all, as the old adage goes "hard work never hurt anyone". Perhaps there is more behind *karoshi* than just hard work.

Some would argue that the distinct Japanese system of hard work is a favourable concept; however, it can and does put workers under extreme pressures and fosters feelings of helplessness. If workers are not happy at work, and are not able to realise their wants from their professional lives, then they are unhappy for a large part of their daily life. The work of Dr Walter Tubbs (Tubbs 1993) has centred on mind-body interactions, and his research on *karoshi* yields some interesting insights. He states:

> *"I believe the real cause of* karoshi *is helplessness, and the related mental states of hopelessness, depression and despair.... I believe that stress death is primarily a matter of attitude and mental causality... [death is not only from overwork] but from intractable despair at being trapped in a vicious cycle over which they have no control, and from which there is no chance of change or escape."* (Tubbs 1993)

In a statement that has upset and offended many traditionalist Japanese, Akio Morita, the flamboyant individual running the Sony Corporation, suggested that companies should begin to give back more to their employees and society. Speaking publicly, he drew attention to the fact that Japanese companies have abandoned their consideration of their employees in pursuit of profit and competitiveness. Morita stated that company's financial contribution to the community is low: only 0.33% of pre-tax profits in 1989, compared with a corresponding contribution of 1.55% in the USA.

It is not only a more humane way of treating staff that is needed, but a much more ethical and productive way of working. The associated costs of stress-induced illnesses are huge, and prevention is always better than the cure. The Pacific Mutual Life Insurance Company has calculated the cost of replacing a high-level corporate executive, because of ill health, is between $250 000 and $500 000. In an extreme case, what is the price of a death?

# Deming Revisited

The work of W. Edwards Deming has been diffusing throughout the world's organisations since the 1950s. He came from a middle-class background, with his educational roots in manufacturing, through a BSc in engineering. He further went on to obtain a PhD in mathematics and physics at Yale University before serving as a statistical consultant to Japanese industry, which at the time was trying to recover from the war. He once remarked that he would like to be remembered as "someone who spent his life trying to keep America from committing suicide". Deming states (Deming 1982) that:

*"...defining quality is to translate future needs of the user into measurable characteristics so that a product can be easily designed and turned out to give satisfaction at a price the user will pay."*

In contrast to Taylor, Deming was not solely concerned with production methods, but also placed strong emphasis on the customer's needs, and advocated returning the quality control function to the worker. To Deming, the customer should always be remembered, and quality is defined by the customer alone.

The approach is a sensible one. Customers should be viewed as integral to the business, not just a separate entity; every business that is to survive into the next quarter understands this, but only a few have viewed other colleagues, functions and departments as part of the customer chain. These groups of workers are the internal customers in the organisation; without customer response, one cannot establish whether value has been added, or cost, through the chain. Quality is everyone's business. There needs to be a movement away from supervisory approaches to quality control, towards a situation where workers themselves accept responsibility and are accountable for their own performance. Indeed, Deming believes that 85% of production problems are due to management.

Deming successfully incorporated historical management principles into his approach, and emphasised that leadership should not be authoritarian.

## THE FOURTEEN PRINCIPLES

Deming identified fourteen principles, derived from his experiences in Japan, that he believed formed the basis of transformation of a company into a "quality organisation" (see Table 8.4). It is easy to see why Tom Gilb has identified many of the principles of human-centred systems as having been set out by Deming. Powerful ideas do not have to be new.

*Table 8.4   Deming's fourteen precepts of quality*

| | The fourteen principles |
|---|---|
| Create constancy of purpose for improvement. | The emphasis should be on the future, and needs to involve innovation, continuous improvement and effective resource identification. |
| Adopt the new philosophy. | Transformation of the organisation, instilling the idea that mistakes (commonly accepted) are not the natural course. Management must lead the way. |
| Cease dependence on inspection. | Inspection to improve quality is too late and implies processes that are inherently flawed. The focus should not be on quantity with the knowledge that quality control inspectors will identify mistakes. |
| End the practice of awarding business on price alone. | Price has little meaning without an indication of the quality: the lowest bidder has not usually emphasised quality. |
| Improve constantly and forever every process. | Quality needs to be built into the process and continually monitored by statistical techniques (which themselves must be continually improved) so that problems are corrected as they occur. |
| Institute training on the job. | Managers need to learn the processes and appreciate variation. New workers need to learn their procedures thoroughly. |
| Adopt and institute leadership. | The job of management is not supervision, but leadership: barriers to improvement should be removed and the overall system managed. |
| Drive out fear. | Management must drive out sources of fear and focus on change. |
| Break down barriers. | Workers in different areas (research, design, sales etc.) should not set up competing and conflicting goals. Cross-functional teams break down barriers and facilitate co-operation. |
| Eliminate slogans and exhortations. | Slogans on improvement don't make any improvements. |
| Eliminate numerical quotas. | Quotas go against quality in productions and focus on quantity. |
| Remove barriers that rob people of pride of workmanship. | Barriers (including performance appraisal and merit pay) prevent workers doing a good job and frustrate them. |
| Institute a program of education and self-improvement. | Organisations not only need good people, but people improving with education: study directed at immediate need is not always the wisest course. |
| Involve everybody to accomplish the transformation. | A course of action should be planned, tested, and corrections made. |

# Deming vs. Taylor: The Differences

Deming and Taylor had common backgrounds; both worked in factory environments and took an engineering approach.

Taylor believed that scientific methods should totally replace personal judgement about work, and distilled his ideas into the text of his book *The Principles of Scientific Management* (Taylor, 1911). His focus was highly quantitative, while Deming emphasised qualitative measures.

During the period of the industrial revolution, the quantitative approach increased efficiency and productivity; the systematic approach was appropriate during that time in history. Today's environment requires a change from simply managing by numbers; this method, and others like it, are no longer relevant to complex international markets. We cannot drive business into the future by, as it were, looking into the rear-view mirror.

Maintaining quality is a separate entity in Taylor's eyes; the company requires an independent organisational function employing inspectors to identify and root out mistakes, with ownership of the process remaining with management. Deming, on the other hand, advocates a return of responsibility to the worker, so that employee pride may reappear, and believes in building quality into the process, monitored and improved by the worker during the production process; performance improvement is a continuous goal and does not reach an optimal peak (Deming 1986). A summary of the differences between the respective views of Taylor and Deming is provided in Table 8.9 (Knouse and Carson 1992).

*Table 8.5    Taylor and Deming – a summary of differences*

|  | Taylor | Deming |
|---|---|---|
| Quantity vs. quality productivity. | Productivity as numerical counts. | Increased quality reduces costs and increases efficiency. |
| Quality control and performance. | Quality control as after-the-fact inspection. | Quality built into the process and continuously improved. |
| Participation. | Ownership of the process and innovation by management. | Ownership of the process returned to the worker, worker suggestions for improvement. |
| Human nature and motivation. | Workers as intrinsically unmotivated. | Workers intrinsically motivated. |
| Individual vs. the group. | Orientation toward the individual worker; improve individual productivity; teamwork thwarts individual improvement. | Orientation toward the workers' group; improve group co-operation; individualism reduces teamwork. |
| Unions. | Management must control work processes; bargaining interferes with scientific management. | Workers should control processes; unions are ambivalent. |

# THE HUMAN ELEMENT

The Taylorist approach forces workers to function along set paths in order to maximise scientifically calibrated processes, thus killing individual initiative; the worker is viewed as being intrinsically demotivated. Taylor was convinced that workers habitually "soldiered", i.e. deliberately withheld effort. Many union leaders denounced Taylorism as a technique for attempting to transform humans into machines, focusing on specialisation and decreasing the need for skilled craftsmen. Pay and promotion incentive mechanisms were built to encourage individualism (Taylor's overall approach is individualistic in nature), and group interaction was discouraged because of its dysfunctional nature.

In contrast, Deming believed in the power of the group and the co-operative efforts needed in organisations. His approach to quality management concerns solidarity, equality and security, which help to obtain the most out of the worker; Deming had faith in the individual.

## TQM AND TAYLORISM

TQM has the potential for creating significant competitive advantage; just mentioning the term conjures up images of highly efficient and competitive Japanese organisations that have gained significant segments of world markets, especially in automotive manufacture. Why then do we see numerous American organisations abandoning millions of dollars of investment in TQM projects, and other "Japanese" management techniques, because of their inappropriateness? One would immediately suggest that it is due to improper implementation.

The birth of the quality movement can be attributed to individuals like Deming, and Juran, as discussed earlier in the chapter. This is the widely accepted view, but there are some alternative strands of thought that centre on the theory that the Japanese developed and refined the technique before Deming arrived on the scene. The study of Taylor's work (his publications sold by the million in Japan in translation, as has already been mentioned in Chapter 2) and the study of Ford's production paradigm helped to develop modern TQM theory (Womack *et al.* 1990).

It can indeed be argued that the implementation of TQM is a direct form of introducing Taylorism, and that facets of the TQM approach, like *kaizen* empowerment (see below) and teamworking, support Taylor's prescriptions on organisation theory. Much depends on how the philosophy is applied.

An important aspect of TQM is the process of continuous improvement or *kaizen*, which allows for freedom for the worker and groupworking. In some applications the technique is highly regimented and standardised, where tasks are regulated and enforced, having been examined by time-and-motion studies, in a manner reminiscent of Taylorism. Examples of the process are numerous. One proponent of the TQM approach, Nissan, cited by Imai states (Imai 1986) that

> *"... efforts in (reducing work time) included employing the work-factor method and standardising virtually every motion workers made in performing their tasks ... management tells the workers that the SOP (standard operating procedure) is an absolute standard to which they should strictly conform until it is improved."*

Detailed specifications originate from management and are then given to workers for comment and "continuous approval"; this is a little different from a more participatory process where from the outset workers have a say in their work environment. This continuous improvement in the process, this looking for a best way of performing the task, eliminates the slack time a worker may have in a highly directed work process, and may cause problems should something go wrong (like when a team member is unwell, has a sore arm, etc.). The elimination of buffer stock, a common aspect of TQM in manufacturing, exacerbates the problem, so that overtime has to be worked to attain production targets. One team member working in a plant where TQM has been implemented states (Adler 1993):

*"Standardised work is a joke as far as I can see. We're supposed to go to management and tell them when we have extra seconds to spare. Why should I do that when all that will happen is that they'll take my spare seconds away and work me even harder then before ... I'm no fool."*

Groupworking has in fact been used to transfer control and coercion from management to team members who are subjected to intense peer pressure. Surveillance is no longer required by a hierarchical control structure, as the task is successfully delegated to fellow team members. Some Japanese firms have pioneered new ways of control, using innovative ways to increase peer pressure and conformity; pressure is facilitated by overt displays of performance and error, showing scheduled production, actual production and worker efficiency ratings for all to observe. Lights and buzzers also alert fellow members when operators have difficulties in working at the assembly line rate of flow. Absences, which put strain on the group the absentee belongs to, are displayed on bulletin boards outside each room, colour-coded to represent holiday, emergency, or unexcused non-appearances (Boje and Winsor 1992).

TQM has enjoyed considerable attention, and its implementation is inherently seen as "a good thing". Much here depends on how it is implemented, however, and in what form: many aspects of TQM theory are simply contemporary "stopwatch" techniques that Taylor himself would happily have endorsed. There are dysfunctional aspects of TQM, and the challenge is to understand the implications of implementing what is a deeply integrated programme of social and psychological design.

# Developments and the Way Forward

## Context

The debate on human-centred systems in business cannot be considered in isolation from international political and economic development. The challenge to Taylorism has been, in part, a critique of Western capitalism, which has seen its own place in the world changing. The rival political and economic system of communism has collapsed since 1989, and former Warsaw Pact member countries have been seeking to switch to capitalism, exposing weaknesses in the economic theory which have been hidden through the political and cultural strengths of successful countries.

As William Keegan wrote in *The Spectre of Capitalism* (Keegan 1993):

> *"Capitalism needs to take stock of its differing patterns around the world, and to develop a wider view of economic man than that promoted by the obsession with narrow self-interest that was so fashionable in the 1980s. In the end, the self-interest of the "market economies" is likely to force a wider view upon them."*

We should expect human-centred systems to take different surface forms, in different cultures. Hutton, in *The State We're In* (Hutton 1995) has given a detailed characterisation of the British context. He provides a vivid account of the social class system in post-imperial and post-industrial Britain, and emphasises the importance of reviving the culture of manufacturing. The City of London and financial institutions are blamed for a short-term and financially driven approach, at the expense of the human dimension.

# DEFENCE

A major manufacturing sector has seen its markets, and very survival, under threat. The ending of the cold war has transformed the prospects of the defence sector, in which some experimental human-centred work had been conducted. Defence had been a means of providing state support for industry despite an official policy of *laissez-faire*. Companies had not been subjected to market forces when their work was predominantly for a single customer. They operated in a wholly different quality environment from that of the civil marketplace, with products required to meet complex specifications for short production runs. It is only recently that contracts have changed from a "cost-plus" basis, which gave companies considerable protection for inefficient practices, together with state funding for R&D work. For many defence systems there are new alternative sources of supply from eastern Europe, with comparable quality and considerably lower prices.

# DIVERSIFICATION

Lucas Aerospace provided the focus in the 1970s for radical alternatives to the current product range and methods of working. The case was made, by Mike Cooley and the shop stewards' committee (Cooley 1977), for diversification from defence to more socially useful civil production. Management resisted change, as they saw a satisfactory future in defence. As a result, when the issue of defence diversification arose again in 1990, and attention was given to the civil potential of particular technologies, there was no continuity with previous debates. The company has lost its way, and is in considerable disarray because the quality of some of its products has come under critical scrutiny in the USA.

# CULTURE

The British commercial culture has developed an antipathy to manufacturing. It was the view of the Thatcher government that manufacturing was no longer critical for economic success, and that the future of the British economy would be predominantly in the service industries. In particular, attention has been focused on financial services, an arena in which large profits could be made by trading assets rather than making things.

Michael Porter (Porter 1990) describes Britain as having reached the wealth-driven stage of capitalist development, which he sees as leading to a slow decline in economic prosperity. Earlier stages were driven by investment and innovation, as is still the case with overseas competitors. Porter and Hutton both highlight the distorting effect of financial institutions on business decisions. However, as Hampden-Turner and Trompenaars point out in their study of the cultures of capitalism (Hampden-Turner and Trompenaars 1994):

*"The British, however uncompetitive they are at actually running corporations and making products, are fiercely competitive and verbally moralistic at talking about it."*

## INVESTMENT

Successful manufacturing depends on appropriate investment in plant and machinery to support the exercise of human skill. During years of recession, company cash flows are under pressure, and funds for investment are hard to find, necessitating borrowing. In Britain, banks and financial institutions support companies by lending rather than by equity holdings. They assess lending propositions with reference to conservative assumptions, taking into account the value of assets offered as security, and requiring projections of high returns on investment. A July 1994 report from the Confederation of British Industry (CBI 1994) suggests that companies seek a 20% return on investment, by comparison with a current 3% return on building society accounts. The result is that companies continue with ageing equipment, disadvantaging their employees by comparison with their competitors. More generally, such an approach reinforces short-term thinking by management, as the case for long-term strategic investment will rarely succeed. Hutton has analysed the profound damage this causes to the British economy.

## ACCOUNTANCY

As long as British companies are led by accountants, it is hard to see a prosperous future for human-centred systems in business. The focus on human skill and tacit knowledge sits uneasily with the virtual reality of accountancy, through which managers are distanced from the working environment and offered figures and ratios. Taylorism fits well with the quantitative concerns of accountants, and dovetails neatly with the technology of "executive information systems" and the new competence-based approach of National Vocational Qualifications. Both involve driving towards the future while relying on the rear-view mirror.

## SOCIAL CLASS

The human-centred approach is based on improved communications within flatter, less hierarchical organisations. Experience of skilled work should inform management decisions from cell production level upwards. It is therefore unhelpful if workers and managers come predominantly from different social class backgrounds, and lack a common culture and experience. This has clear implications for education and training.

Charles Handy addresses this social dimension in *The Empty Raincoat* (Handy 1994), seeing a creative tension between equality and inequality in a capitalist democracy:

> *"Capitalism depends on the fundamental principle of inequality - some may do better than others - but will only be acceptable in the long term in a democracy if most people have an equal chance to aspire to that inequality."* (p. 43)

# HUMAN-CENTRED STRATEGY

Rather than adopting a defensive position, or continuing the academic debate on the fringes, we wish to take over the centre ground. We can argue that human-centred systems provide the basis for the next-generation approach to business strategy. Pilot work in recent years provides us with a robust framework that must be addressed at board level across all industrial sectors.

As a starting point we can endorse Handy's restatement (Handy 1994) of the purpose of a company:

> *"The principal purpose of a company is not to make a profit, full stop. It is to make a profit in order to continue to do things, or make things, and to do so ever better and more abundantly."*

Interestingly, he also points to a changing role for organisations, becoming organisers rather than employers as individuals deploy their skills more flexibly. Company mission statements can provide valuable indications of purpose and direction.

## AGILE MANUFACTURING

One approach, favoured by Kidd, is to launch the "Agile Manufacturing" model. An eclectic approach that seeks to draw on business process re-engineering, and which is distinguished from Japanese "lean manufacturing", it is designed to appeal to boardroom strategists, showing the way through to commercial sucess in a highly competitive global environment:

> *"Agile manufacturing implies a revolution in the way we go about designing and implementing manufacturing systems, technologies and organisations, and in the way we conduct our business."* (Kidd 1994: p. viii)

Though Kidd makes reference to the importance of knowledge and skill, one is left with the impression that power would reside with senior managers and consultants, with little more than a token level of consultation with the work-force.

*"Agile manufacturing is primarily a business concept. Its aim is quite simple: to put our enterprises way out in front of our primary competitors. In agile manufacturing, the aim is to combine the organisation, people and technology into an integrated and coordinated whole. The agility that arises from this can be used for competitive advantage, by being able to respond rapidly to changes occurring in the market environment and through the ability to use and exploit a fundamental resource: knowledge."* (Kidd 1994: p. 2)

## IT STRATEGY

The steam has gone out of work on IT for competitive advantage, and the instinct at board level is to refrain from expenditure whenever possible. The step beyond the current enthusiasm for business process re-engineering will be increased outsourcing of IT facilities, potentially making a nonsense of intelligent IT strategy and corporate strategy in general.

If people are the critical resource in the organisation, and IT is becoming a dominant means of communication, as well as the medium for decision making, it would seem vital to retain control of one's own human-centred system. The alternative is for organisations to be remotely run by contractors with competing interests, losing independence to an external imperial force such as EDS. EDS (Electronic Data Systems) was founded by Ross Perot, and is now owned by General Motors. It has been contracted to handle data processing for the British Inland Revenue and many defence projects.

## NETWORKING THE INFORMATION SUPERHIGHWAY

Internet links people, but the technology provides the connection rather than the direction. The same optical links can support multi-media traffic, unidirectional or interactive. Much of the infrastructure is in place. What is needed is a combination of human skill and insight; organisational and corporate strategy; and commitment to access for the wide community. The management approaches from human-centred systems, described earlier, have a central role to play.

## HUMAN-CENTRED COMMUNICATIONS TECHNOLOGIES

We need new case study companies, operating on the national and international stage, and broadening our range of industrial sectors. One such is Snell & Wilcox, a world leader in the technology of broadcast electronics and standards conversion, producing specialist devices to provide real-time conversion of broadcast material between standards. The key resource of the company is human skill in the development and application of advanced technology, drawn from the BBC Research Department, and from broadcasting companies world-wide. The main production facility is housed in a converted watermill in the Hampshire countryside. The cofounder and research director of the company, Roderick Snell, has long been involved with human-centred systems since his days as an academic in Brighton. The chairman and chief executive, David Youlton, with a personal mission to develop British manufacturing capability, is committed to reforming the structure and management of the company to maximise employee involvement and ownership. A cell-based approach is followed by research, development and production teams, pooling their ingenuity for the solution of technical problems. This has to be accompanied by astute financial management, creative communications and an expert international sales team.

A small company has to be perceived by customers and competitors as a major world force in the industry in order to make the critical transition to a medium-sized and then large company. A small company cannot work in isolation, so it is vital to foster an environment in which firms can combine forces on joint projects. This in turn depends on trust and shared values, rather than the narrow pursuit of profit. Appropriate collaboration is a precondition for competitive advantage, as Japanese companies have so frequently demonstrated.

## REGAINING CONTROL

The underlying theme of this book concerns skilled workers regaining control of their work, and an influence over its products. To require flexibility from workers without involving them in decision making is to court failure, and to reinforce the division of labour between manager and managed. In turn this requires a shift in education and training policy and practice to rebuild the central role of skill, which has been lost in the rush for competence. Cultural adjustments are implied, because skill in engineering is seen as applying not just to financial and social engineering, but also to manufacturing.

# Appendices

The following appendices contain full case studies of the organisations referenced in the main body of the book. Each aims to provide a richer and more detailed picture of the points and issues raised where referenced.

# Appendix 1: Volvo, Uddevalla and Kalmar, Sweden

Volvo is regarded as one of the early proponents of a human-centred approach. For sound commercial reasons they implemented a return to a traditional craft approach to work in their factories, allowing teams a level of authority and autonomy over decisions and actions that is elsewhere typically held by senior management.

Senior management in Volvo had been concerned by enormous rates of fluctuation in productivity and high levels of absenteeism. They were convinced that a new type of automobile factory, and related ways of working, were required. At the time of the changes, Volvo was experiencing problems in recruiting new personnel, within a very tight and demanding labour market. The company is Sweden's largest organisation, generating 8% of gross national product, with over 80% of its passenger cars being exported.

In 1974 Volvo opened a pioneering factory in Kalmar, followed by a plant in Uddevalla 15 years later. The philosophy and belief behind these plants was that working life has to be adapted to people rather than to technology. The two plants represent a 20-year period in which Volvo has humanised and democratically inspired unions, managers and shop-floor workers.

## A Holistic Approach

Uddevalla, perhaps more than Kalmar, exemplified the early applications of the human-centred approach. Some fundamental features of the Volvo approach may be outlined as follows:

- Both plants, as well as the company overall, were committed to considering employees as their most important assets. A strong working relationship was encouraged and nurtured between unions and management.
- Production teams were established. The move away from Tayloristic concepts and ideals was deliberate, and radical at the time. Responsibility was restored to the individual or team. Uddevalla had no reworking area, and corrections were returned to the team, providing a channel for feedback; the responsibility for quality was governed by the team. The plants were built to attract Swedish workers, with an environment that they would want to work in, rather than one that they were obliged to enter in order to earn money. Typically a working group, essentially a factory within a factory, consisting of 10 workers, built the entire car.
- The Fordist assembly line was completely abolished, and teams of workers took full responsibility for assembling cars. Each team was afforded the autonomy to decide their own schedules, work pace and overtime requirements. Long work cycles were popular, as they reduced boredom and stress. Team leaders were elected by the group, and often the role was rotated between different members of the team. A supervisor, in the traditional sense, was not required, and first-line management was eliminated completely.
- Training and continued education were deemed as important to the well-being of workers, and final output; as new skills were learned, workers' wages increased respectively. This provided an incentive for workers to build upon, and to supplement their existing knowledge. New workers spent their first sixteen months developing basic skills and then progressed to building upon these core skills, by working within teams of experienced personnel. Not only were technical education and skills important, but managerial and interpersonal skills were also stressed. The distinct stages of learning led to an individual gaining a "master level", which represented the skills required to assemble an entire car. In general there was recognition that learning and competence were not things just for an élite group in top management, but should be applied universally.
- The Uddevalla environment was different from that of a traditional factory. It possessed a clean and bright interior with little noise and movement. Aesthetically, the plant had realised Volvo's goal of creating a pleasant and stress-free working environment. Ergonomically, specially designed tools, practices and machines were provided, catering for gender differences; for example, team members would spend up to 80% of their time working in an upright position.
- Workers were asked to seek out improvements in the way processes were run and encouraged to provide feedback and comments. They were in a good position to comment on many aspects of the cycle, as each member of a group would be engaged in all aspects of building a car. The workers became involved with the wishes of the customer, and group fusion made production objectives a key goal.

# Uddevalla – Ahead of its Time?

The new form of work organisation that Volvo was building centred on creating a "new type of professional", built upon the established and successful European system of craftsmen and guilds, inherently with apprentices and masters. The goal was to move away from intrinsically dehumanising work organisation and narrow tasks that epitomised the Taylorist way. In the true Swedish tradition, the quality of working life was improved for all involved with building Volvo vehicles.

The approach did not escape its critics. They pointed to the fact that Uddevalla was developed at a time when Volvo operated in a protected market without the threat, for its niche, from the Japanese car makers. At the time the company was selling all it could make, and the constraint of the day was the tight labour market conditions; the Uddevalla plant was built to make Swedish workers want to work in it, and consequently the processes that shaped it were labour-driven rather than productivity-driven.

Many policies that Volvo put into place within the Uddevalla plant were declared by its critics to be more akin to abandonment rather than empowerment. Detailed methods and standards passed to Uddevalla, from the more traditional plants, were ignored as workers built new procedures. Established ways were ignored, which is not necessarily a bad thing, but critics have pointed to the fact that very little communication passed between different teams and functions. Formal communication paths were not established, although informal networks grew and flourished between teams and individuals.

These criticisms are not totally without significance. Volvo was pioneering a new way of working, and was far-sighted enough to invest in the learning process of a more balanced approach; an important element of this was the acceptance that mistakes would be made, and a subsequent learning process would follow. Researchers studying the Uddevalla approach support this view; thus Rehder states:

> *"It is my impression that Uddevalla's management is well aware of the complexity of group dynamics, leadership development and intrateam technology transfer as well as the design and development of their individual and group incentive systems. Management therefore appeared to be following a strategy of slow and patient experimentation, given the new ground they are breaking and the paucity of theoretical knowledge in this complex area."* (Rehder 1992)

Christian Berggren, an associate professor at the Royal Institute of Technology in Sweden, has also studied the Volvo approach in detail. He cites the comments of a shop manager (Berggren 1994):

> *"We had to learn so many things from scratch, starting with a process of unlearning, getting rid of previous conceptions and behaviour. Only in September 1992 did we find an organisation suited to our production concept. We also introduced a new programme for leadership development, which was essential... The first session of the*

*programme took place in November, on the same day the close-down decision was announced."*

Other criticisms argued that, in automotive manufacture, short work cycles and continuous scrutinisation of possible improvements in processes are essential. Uddevalla's cycle times were long when compared to those of similar Japanese and US firms. Standardised tools, and statistical procedures to highlight these possible improvements, were lacking in the Uddevalla cycle and work methodology. Instead, Volvo had developed a new set of tools for a new type of workforce; as well as the nurturing of close group work, there was an excellent balance of equal opportunity, with targets of 40% of workers in Uddevalla being women, 25% of both genders being under 25 and the same proportion being over 45. The belief was that a balanced team with experience and judgement would lead to greater social harmony.

Interestingly, most of the frequent visitors to the Uddevalla plant were executives from Japanese companies, who widely utilised standard accepted tools and approaches. One can criticise Volvo for not marketing the Uddevalla concept enough; its working practices were excellent and ground-breaking, but other aspects of its organisation left room for improvement. For instance, in more recent times we have seen the emergence of human production processes being cited as a critical selling point with the General Motors Saturn vehicle, yet Uddevalla was significantly more advanced than the GM project.

Today, the emphasis in most economies world-wide is a challenge to recruit and retain educated personnel, capable and receptive to further learning and skills enhancement. The tools of production continue to change, with increasing emphasis on labour requirements as the scarce resource. Volvo, and the Swedish market in general, faced this issue before some of its European partners; it was forced to adapt to the new changed conditions and began to foster a more humanistic and balanced approach to attract workers.

Volvo's approach of providing an attractive workplace for potential recruits certainly worked; Uddevalla boasted a rate of 6% for both absenteeism and turnover in 1991, compared with the average of 20% for the Swedish market as a whole.

# The Current Status

In November 1992 Volvo announced that the Uddevalla and Kalmar plants would be closed, in 1993 and spring 1994 respectively. It was stressed that this was not due to poor performance; in fact the Kalmar plant was already operating at higher productivity and quality levels than those at Volvo's more traditional main plant, Torslanda. The reasons given for the closure, as outlined by Volvo's public affairs department to the second author, are provided below (Peer 1994):

*"With its current high level of surplus capacity, the automotive industry is very vulnerable.... Even Japanese car manufacturers are beginning to experience falling profits. Sales have fallen in many of Volvo's main markets, not least in Sweden, where the total market has fallen by a third since the late eighties. Our total deficit for the past three years amounts to more than SEK [Swedish Crowns] 4500 million. These figures explain much of the background to the closures.... We expect to sell 230 000–255 000 cars per year. In Torslanda and Ghent we have the capacity for about 300 000; the two plants are complete with body shops, paintshops and assembly, unlike Kalmar and Uddevalla, which are occupied solely with final assembly.*

*It cannot be over-emphasised that the decision to close the Kalmar and Uddevalla plants was essential from the view of capacity. It does not represent an evaluation of different production methods. Both plants have provided a great deal of experience...we will be assimilating and applying this expertise as extensively as possible. Some ideas have already been introduced in production at Torslanda.... All calculations have been studied by unions and no criticisms have been expressed."*

Was Uddevalla ahead of its time? Certainly the plant was evolving and learning continuously, driven by different business, competitive and environmental issues. Throughout this period, the central theme and philosophy behind the plant remained intact. Despite the success of the plant, it is still the subject of wild and usually inaccurate rumours, further fuelled since Volvo announced its closure – which provide a stark display of society's slow acceptance of changing work structures and processes.

One cannot help but question the public rhetoric Volvo provided for closing the two plants, and the financial figures are also somewhat suspect. As Åke Sandberg, a research director at the Swedish Centre For Working Life, has outlined, several anomalies exist (Sandberg 1994):

- Torslanda, the main Volvo plant, boasted 42 work hours per car, yet just before the closure of Uddevalla, the equivalent statistic in that plant was 32.8 work hours (plus an additional 6 for white-collar work). Indeed, an indication of Uddevalla was the example of one worker building an entire car in just 10 hours: significantly less than the Japanese level of 25 work hours.

- It is questionable why the Swedish Metal Workers' Union did not defend the Uddevalla and Kalmar plants. Perhaps some of the reasoning can be explained by the concentration of management and union power at the Gothenburg and Torslanda plants, giving them a numerical advantage in votes. Whatever the reason, the reputation of the union has always been one of promoting solidarity and good work procedures; the closure of the plants signifies a coalition undermining this attitude.

- The united Renault–Volvo future represented a clash of industrial work style and ideas. It is not without significance that a consultants' report for the French government criticised the setup of Kalmar and Uddevalla.

Had Uddevalla survived, it certainly possessed the potential to evolve further, and develop new ways to continue to compete on an international basis, while still retaining its democratic, worker-centred features. Many of the experiences and lessons learnt from the Uddevalla and Kalmar plants have already been incorporated successfully in the Torslanda plant, specifically in ergonomic improvements, more comprehensive assembly sequences and increased teamwork initiatives. The resulting developments can be accredited to the introduction of these approaches, but one can question if the experiences learnt at Uddevalla and Kalmar will die over time, while the new culture at Volvo centres upon the adoption of "lean manufacturing" in its Japanese context. This would be an unfortunate and ironic turnaround for two plants whose way of working attracted attention from Japanese companies and provided learning experiences for them (Adler and Cole 1993, Rehder 1992, Berggren 1994).

# Appendix 2: ESPRIT 1217 (1199) – Human-Centred CIM

## The BICC Need

It was during the early 1980s that a subsidiary of the BICC Group, a multinational organisation with a turnover in excess of four billion pounds, identified a specific need. The need was focused around smaller subsidiary organisations (SMEs) in general. The BICC Group included some two dozen of these smaller organisations, mainly in the manufacturing sector, as subsidiary companies with some similar characteristics, specifically a turnover of approximately £10 million and a workforce of approximately 200 persons.

Recent years had seen significant sums of money and resources invested in these organisations, in an attempt to make them more competitive. Large amounts of investment centred on "technological solutions" and large, flexible manufacturing systems were installed alongside robotic assembly lines. Technology was viewed as the panacea, but the returns on these investments were somewhat less than optimal in each case, where large capital investment had been made and returns were significantly less than anticipated.

The results tended to support Professor Voss's findings (Voss 1993), which indicated that almost all the installations were technically successful, but that only 14% of those investments improved the business in an competitive manner. This poor rate of return was identified and, within BICC, a taskforce was assembled in order to ascertain the reasons why, and to recommend steps to remedy the situation. BICC were farsighted enough to realise that although timescales were of importance, there was an immediate need for success, and what was required immediately was that the overall trend should be halted and reversed in time. The possibility of turning a loss-making venture into a profit within a year was idealistic and unrealistic, because the downward trend had been prevalent for some years, and it was anticipated that a reversal would take place within two to five years.

A survey of the group was undertaken in order to establish the principal problems for the companies concerned. The aim was not to focus on individual problems, but rather to establish whether there were any generic problems affecting the group as a whole. Extensive surveys of companies were undertaken in the UK, continental Europe, Canada and Australia, yielding three generic problems:

- Product lead times.
- Customer satisfaction.
- Work-in-progress levels.

It was found that all the companies exhibited, to some extent, long lead times and poor due-date performance, and possessed high work in progress levels. It was then felt that all three issues were interlinked, and could be solved if lead times could be effectively reduced. This would put emphasis on principal areas and have subsequent knock-on effects through the organisation.

During the world-wide internal survey of the Group of BICC companies, an unusual correlation was identified between successful projects and numbers of meetings. It transpired that the more successful projects had far more meetings between both management and shop-floor personnel than comparable failed projects. This went against the time's conventional wisdom, which suggested that the more meetings there were, the more confusion there would be! Obviously this was not borne out in practice.

Around this time, during the 1980s, a number of "accidents" occurred when installing some large computer-based systems within companies. All the accidents pointed to a lack of understanding of what the systems would do, and an ignorance of changed work styles and practices by those concerned. In contrast, those applications that were more successful consisted of different teams of people contributing to a greater extent to the overall "solution".

It was at this time that BICC encountered the term "Human-centred Systems" and two years later participated in the ESPRIT Project; it was a sensible and natural progression, because the project fitted in with the BICC task force team's efforts.

# The Research Project – Human-Centred Computer-integrated Manufacturing (CIM)

One of the best-known cases of human-centred research is a project funded by the Commission of the European Communities (CEC). The purpose of the

ESPRIT project 1217 (1199), which commenced in May 1986, was to design a human-centred, computer-integrated system for manufacturing, on the premise that a CIM system will be more efficient, economical, robust and flexible if a person is directly in charge than a comparable unmanned system. It was probably the first European project to bring together the three European traditions of human-centredness: British, Scandinavian and German. The principal objectives of the project were to

- establish criteria for the design of human-centred CIM systems;
- establish their economic and commercial competitiveness;
- achieve a better shop-floor environment and better working practises;
- achieve a high level of flexibility and robustness in CIM systems;
- define the training for a new type of multi-skilled worker;
- demonstrate at a production site that there is a better means of organising manufacturing, especially suited to Europe.

The project involved the design of a manufacturing system that would

- enhance human skill and ingenuity rather than attempt to replace it;
- follow the principles of sociotechnical system design, where the technical and social aspects of the organisation system are jointly optimised;
- follow a user orientation in system design such that functionality is considered from the users' viewpoint rather than the system designers'.

The human-centred approach was particularly appropriate to small batch production environments (which is the most common manufacturing environment in Europe), as it incorporates the necessary system flexibility.


# Project Participants


Partners in three countries took part in the project: the UK, Denmark and West Germany. Denmark's main focus was the design of a human-centred sketching module attached to a conventional CAD system (see Figure A2.1). Germany took care of the design of a human-centred, computer-aided production planning (CAPP) system. The discussion centres on the UK's involvement, and Britain was interested in the design of a human-centred computer-aided manufacturing (CAM) system, consisting of

- factory-planning software;
- a production-scheduling system;
- cell-scheduling software;

- Lathe-control software for two advanced computer-numerically controlled (CNC) lathes.

Several UK organisations participated in the project, namely

- **Greater London Enterprise:** project managers and prime contractors.
- **RDP Technology:** developers of the cell-scheduling software and control software for the CNC machines.
- **Rolls-Royce,** helicopter division: installation site of the CNC machines.
- **BICC Technologies:** developers of the factory-planning and production-scheduling systems.
- **ITT Sealectro:** installation site for the planning and scheduling systems.
- **University of Manchester Institute of Science and Technology** (UMIST): originally providing the social science contribution.
- **MRC/ESRC** Social and Applied Psychology Unit at Sheffield University (as sub-contractors to UMIST): provision of input on organisational aspects of system design and implementation.

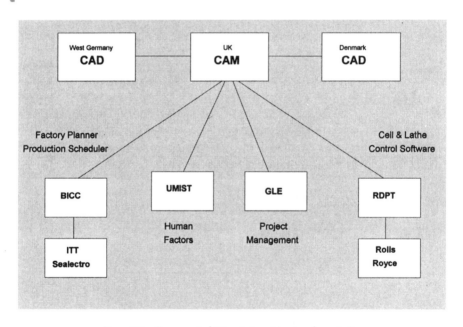

*Figure A2.1    Human-centred CIM project: participants and organisation*

All the software for the CAM operation was designed to offer as much autonomy for the users as possible. The major difference in approach, when compared with traditional projects, was that this project was concerned with building software that would allow people to perform their jobs better by providing more information and control, rather than building systems to perform their jobs.

# Findings

Some of the findings from this project include the following:

- The interdisciplinary cooperation between social scientists and engineers may be difficult at times, but it is always refreshing and innovative; this is important.
- The need to specify the technical hardware in the project proposal already limited the project by actually giving it a technology-centred start, but it was important that the hardware should be purchased in the first six months, if a fully functioning system was to be delivered within three years.
- Users should be involved from an early stage and their views and comments should influence the design.
- The concept of human-centred CIM has to be introduced diplomatically. Giving control to the shop-floor operators and involving them in the process of development and implementation of a new system may seem unfavourable or even dangerous to the management involved.
- A generic change in attitude has to take place, with all people involved acknowledging benefits of this approach. For example, operator motivation and job satisfaction are more likely to have an effect on productivity than machine utilisation statistics.
- Bureaucratic management fails to take advantage of the skill and initiative of the workforce.
- Attitudes embedded in the scientific and technological culture make it difficult to accept human purpose. To the engineer and technological worker, a system that relies on the existence of human skill, and particularly manual skill, will appear defective and incomplete. Only knowledge that is explicit and definable is accepted: this can be embodied in textbooks, transmitted to new generations and used as a basis of further advance.
- The dream of a workerless factory may never be achieved, as scientists are unable to incorporate human purpose into machines.

  *"No machine which we can build can have the purpose of keeping the production working.... Machines do not care whether they work or not, and we do not know how to incorporate that purpose. So machines will work well until something occurs which was not envisaged in their design."*
  (Rosenbrock 1989)

- To achieve a fruitful collaboration between social scientists and technologists, it is necessary for each discipline to respect the other's point of view. For technologists, the problem is one of including a social dimension in the decision-making process. This means the inclusion of thought as to whether the user will be subordinated to the technicalities of the final system, or actually use the system as a tool as a creative part of the production process. For social scientists generalities have, if necessary, to be made specific in the face of hard constraints, i.e. time, economics and technical feasibility.

- The use of language is an important and critical consideration. Engineers are not versed and comfortable with theoretical and philosophical treatises; the terminology is difficult to understand and comprehend. As Gottschalch states, drawing conclusions from the experience (Gottschalch 1992):

  "*one need not proceed in such a clumsy way as we attempted in ESPRIT 1217; in lengthy lectures social scientists treated engineers to a collection of abstract and demanding philosophical theories; the latter listened patiently and politely, and their complete lack of comprehension and the lack of backtalk was mistaken for enlightenment and agreement.*"

# Appendix 3:
# The MOPS Programme

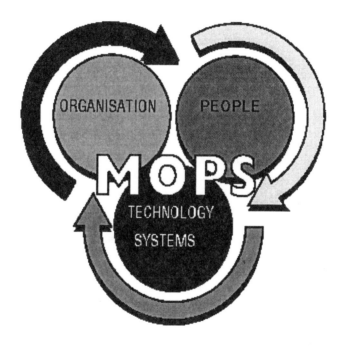

Figure A3.1

The DTI's Manufacturing Organisation People and Systems (MOPS) Initiative was launched in April 1991 to help industry, in particular SMEs, to manage change within their manufacturing environment. This was facilitated by supporting collaborative industrial R&D projects that involved organisational and people issues. The focus was very much on the R&D of strategies, support tools and methods to assist UK industry to improve manufacturing system design practices and introduce new organisational and management structures. As well as BESTMAN, which we consider separately in Appendix 4, the programme supported five other projects:

- **CIRCA:** Continuous Improvement: Research for Competitive Advantage.
- **DESTINY:** The Development of a Software Tool for the Analysis and Improvement of Organisational Structures in Manufacturing Industry.
- **IMOCIM:** Intelligent Management of Change in Manufacturing.
- **OSISTIM:** Objective Systems to Implement Successfully Team Working in Manufacturing.
- **TIM:** Methods and Tools for Reinforcing and Developing Teamwork in Manufacturing.

# CIRCA

CIRCA was a two-year research project set up in 1991 to investigate how the concept and practice of continuous improvement (CI) can be introduced and sustained in UK industry; it represented a collaboration between industrial and academic partners. CI consists of making many small improvements, continuously at all levels, in an organisation over a sustained period of time. It has been in existence for many years and took off in the late 1940s with the rebuilding of the Japanese manufacturing industry. The introduction and successful management of CI are not automatic, and it has been relatively slow to spread in the UK.

The purpose of the project was to devise a generic framework for setting up and maintaining CI in any firm, and in support of this a "toolbox" of techniques, methodologies and paper/computer-based tools were developed. This was achieved by research with a small group of companies, including SMEs, where the generic framework and toolbox were being piloted, as well as large experienced user firms. The introduction and experimentation of CI projects are building up a picture of how CI works best in practice. Results and experiences were shared through the CIRCA network of interested parties as well as seminars, workshops and quarterly bulletins.

# DESTINY

This project developed a diagnostic PC software tool to assist manufacturing companies in the identification, analysis and improvement of:

- Present organisational structures and the way that they really work.
- Interpersonal working relationships and problems.
- Peer group working relationships and problems.
- Key organisational issues.

The tool allows organisational structures to be modelled and refined before being implemented, offering the opportunity to experiment with organisational change on paper first as opposed to with people. Using modified versions of two existing methodologies, their application to manufacturing aspects having been strengthened, an integrated tool is to be implemented.


# IMOCIM


The IMOCIM project developed a methodology for the management of change in manufacturing, which was being embodied in a knowledge-based system (KBS). The framework of initiating and managing change was developed, as well as the attributes of World Class Manufacturing Performance (WCM); the philosophy of the project was that if an enterprise was to survive in the long term it must aim for this performance.

The methodology took a holistic approach, where individual client solutions are generated, taking into account people, organisation, systems and technology in the context of WCM performance. The consortium was led by Euristics Ltd, a company that specialises in KBS applications, development and consultancy. Other partners were two consultancy firms – Silicon Bridge Ltd and Cheshire Henbury.


# OSISTIM


In this project a consortium was established to undertake the objective measurement of individual attributes necessary for successful team working, and the results both productively and culturally achieved, with a brief to seek and validate such measurement systems.

A programme was set up to design and implement objective systems of individual and collective assessment in order to assist companies to implement team-based organisations. The measurement systems to provide data in these innovative team structures were designed by Selection Research Ltd and encompassed the following:

- structured interviews to identify those who fit and have the potential for success in a team-working environment;
- peer rating assessment systems integrated with the interviews to measure the productivity and contribution of team members;
- Managing Attitudes for Productivity (MAP) surveys to measure the attitudes and morale of team members, and to inform management on progress towards the new team-based organisational culture.

# TIM

The rationale behind TIM was to develop tools to assess achievements, after the introduction of "teams". The project involved developing, testing, evaluating and disseminating methods and tools to help manufacturers. Through collaborative work, practical problems of reconciling teamwork had been identified, and 20 to 30 small companies who had expressed interest in the project were being used to test these conclusions. The project had specific R&D objectives:

- To produce an analysis of the range of technical and organisational change issues faced by companies that make a move towards team-work.
- To develop a methodology applicable to a variety of company circumstances, which can be used by companies to assess what they have achieved.
- To develop a range of methods and tools for tackling specific areas where development is commonly required, and where satisfactory approaches have not yet been developed.

# Appendix 4: BESTMAN

Project BESTMAN – Best Practice Cellular Manufacture – was one of the six MOPS projects. The project aimed to identify and map the methods and procedures utilised in six collaborating companies, taking into account the people, organisational and technical issues. It researched/identified the following:

- The business organisation required to make best use of cellular manufacturing.
- The design of manufacturing cells themselves.
- The best way of scheduling work in them.
- The degree of authority given to the shop floor.
- The educational, training and development needs.
- It identified the problems encountered and made recommendations for the future.

The project planned to research, test and study the design and economics of manufacturing cells used across different manufacturing sectors. It was to review the communication needs, skills, ideal cell mix and potential product flexibility that could be achieved. The focus was on people at all levels in the organisation. A top-down view was taken at the strategic level, while a bottom-up view was to be taken at the tactical level. The project took into consideration the needs of different companies, but concentrated on common features valid across different sectors. The outcome was to be a set of procedures, methods and application plans, backed by the appropriate level of technological support.

The consortium consisted of six manufacturing companies, together with A. T. Kearney and Human Centred Systems Ltd. The six industrial companies (GEC Engineering, DeVilbiss Ransburg, Harrison Industries, Temco, Drexel and Kysor) provided a cross-section of manufacturing industry. A. T. Kearney brought a breadth of skills and proven financial practices to the project, and was able to evaluate the economic factors. It developed the "Best of the Best" benchmarking programme, with a questionnaire that enables an organisations' operations to be calibrated relative to world-class standards. Human Centred Systems Ltd brought proven cell-based manufacturing research experience.

# The Multi-level Generic Model

Following initial data acquisition, a multi-level BESTMAN generic model was constructed by the first author, showing the stages through which an organisation has to progress to be designated as a "Best Cell-based Manufacturing Enterprise". The stages are listed below.

## SURVIVAL LEVEL

This is characterised by late deliveries; poor quality; long cycle time; poor relationships with customers and/or suppliers; poor teamwork, ownership and initiative; unclear strategy and focus.

## REACTIVE LEVEL

Here there is some response to priorities such as customers and products; however, there also exist islands of conflicting groups or departments; isolated, conflicting systems and processes; and several strategies.

## DIRECTIVE LEVEL

At this level a strategy is determined; priorities and goals are established; communications are promoted; conflict is brought out into the open; and "hit squads" are created.

## PROACTIVE LEVEL

Squads now become teams; people continue to set goals and seek approval for initiatives; integration is becoming the norm; customer and supplier focus is paramount; knowing your customer becomes a culture.

## EMPOWERMENT LEVEL

We now find shortened chains of command; greater trust and responsibility; the elimination of non-value added activities; and a secure, proud culture.

## BESTMAN BEST-OF-BEST

At this highest level we find continuous improvement in all areas (organisational, people and technological). The key issue was the facilitation of transitions between these stages, using implementation tools, including paper-based and software-based tools. Use was made of tools, such as the ACiT scheduling system, which had been developed under the ESPRIT project described above. Links between the MOPS projects facilitated the exchange and exploitation of new tools.

# Appendix 5:
# ITW DeVilbiss Ransburg

ITW DeVilbiss Ransburg was one of the partner companies in the BESTMAN project. Based in Poole, DeVilbiss manufactures spray guns and booths, complete with robotics of which 40% are exported. It produces the equipment that not only sprays conventional paints, but also diverse products such as equipment that sprays flavouring onto potato crisps. Although it operates within a highly competitive environment it is regarded as providing a world standard in its product range.

The company was very much in the forefront of the project, and were spearheading the programme. It had already made significant progress towards a balanced approach, integrating organisation, technology and people, which had begun in 1990. The factory had been divided into sixteen cells and had increased the qualification levels and pay of the people in those cells. The approach had been that of developing one or two cells at a time. Already well on their way to Best Practice Cellular Manufacture, the company wanted to move towards a more responsive and flexible organisation where ideas for improvement were fed "upwards" through the system.

## Objectives

The company has three primary objectives, as follows:

1.  *Reduction of product unit costs.* Growing competition in this market comes from Japanese companies that have already introduced flexible variable products at keen prices. To prepare for a defence of market share, profitability and competitive edge had both to be improved.
2.  *Improvements in building quality.* Quality demanded by customers was

imperative and continuous improvements were required.
3. *Improvements in customer service.* Although on-time delivery was 90%, the focus was on reducing cycle and response times to facilitate a 48-hour delivery promise.

# Refocusing Strategy

The principal reasons for conducting a major restructuring of the business were to improve customer responsiveness and to reduce inventory levels. Several changes were undertaken, as follows.

## PRODUCT RATIONALISATION

The overall range of products was reduced, with consequential reductions in the number of component parts. This was achieved by analysing their portfolio, and subsequently inactive products were handled by separate operations. A reduced range of options was offered by upgrading lower-level products without adversely impacting price.

## COMPONENT OUTSOURCING

To reduce complexity in the manufacturing operations, an analysis was carried out to identify products that could be outsourced. There was a downside to increasing outsourcing, namely an increase in "raw-material" inventory costs. To compensate for this there was a general downsizing of the operations business and hence costs.

## OPERATIONS BUSINESS FOCUSING

As a result of reducing the range of components it was possible to reorganise the manufacturing activities to improve focus and simplify the overall structure. Manufactured items are now made in sufficient volume to allow resources to be dedicated to the production of specific groups of components in specific cells.

Despite major reorganisation activities in the manufacturing operations of the company, DeVilbiss was successful in achieving BS 5750 quality approval in 1992.

# Implementation

The product range was rationalised, from 3537 saleable items comprising of 7000 components to 1154 saleable items with 2942 components. This enabled the supplier base to be reduced from 404 to 264 and non-strategic components were outsourced, with KANBANs set up with selected suppliers. The reduced range of items enabled dedicated resources for specific cells, the segregation made on the basis of

- High volume;
- Low volume;
- Inactivity.

Factory A, a factory within a factory, dealt with high-volume orders; and because of the stable demand associated with these products the facilities were laid out to cater for just-in-time (JIT) manufacture. Much of the reorganisation was under way when the project began and new procedures were already being established.

Factory B had the same principles applied, and only strategic components were manufactured. Material and manufacturing control systems are still utilised, but these will be simplified in line with the formation of cells. KANBAN systems were introduced, together with an educational and development programme. At the commencement of the project, Factory B still operated using management structures that had been used prior to the reorganisation, and thus gave a reflection of the previous state of the organisation.

Inactive parts were moved into a separate building which is unstaffed until an order is received.

# Personnel Issues

People are naturally inclined to be reluctant to embrace change and maintain the *status quo*, and one of the biggest challenges identified by management was to foster a corporate ethos that encouraged change. The principal characteristic was one of management authority and responsibility being genuinely devolved to cell leaders, who were totally responsible for day-to-day operations. Cell leaders went through a lengthy gestation period before it became clear that they had developed general management capabilities. Subsequently cell leaders developed more rapidly as they had the advantage of the role model of earlier cell leaders. The company was fortunate in having cell leaders who were receptive to change and learning, and were eager to accept the autonomy the cell structure provided.

Once the success of initial cells was noticed by others on the shop floor, a degree of momentum for change developed, and workers demonstrated enthusiasm to begin the process of change. There was an element of a cloning process. The new approach was wholly welcomed by the shop floor, and management felt that this was primarily due to the belief that new approaches would alleviate much of the "frustration in the system". One process used by DeVilbiss to help the acceptance of cells was to abolish the requirement for shop-floor staff to "clock in" if their cell had been established. Others working in the traditional layout still had to punch their card every morning. This in effect gave cell teams a superior status over their peers, and was described by DeVilbiss as one of its "little tricks". It was in effect applied psychology and provided an all-important incentive.

All of this created a problem of ensuring that change was maintained at an appropriate level. If the rate was too slow then enthusiasm was lost, leading to stagnation. If the rate had been too fast then it would have exceeded the ability of the staff, particularly those who provided support services. In practice, the change at DeVilbiss had accelerated as the programme of cell development progressed.

# Systems

DeVilbiss had completely switched off their manufacturing requirements planning (MRP) system by Spring 1993. This process was implemented, module by module, until the organisation did not require the system. There is now virtually no element of materials planning in the traditional sense, and all materials procurement is for simplified storage systems for key components on the shop floor, using bias (or KANBAN), with maximum/minimum-type ordering. Each cell has two bins of components; one is sealed and one is not. Quite simply, if the sealed one has to be opened then a new order is put through. Each cell leader is allowed the freedom to use whichever system they feel is relevant to the operation of their cell.

DeVilbiss no longer keeps inventory statistics on computer. Management's comments are interesting: "if you want to know what is there...go and have a look!... Systems people are effectively slaves to the system and there is a need to prevent them from recording every nut and bolt." The author of these remarks advocates that there is no need for a complex MRP system to do simple jobs that can typically be "...done on Lotus 123".

# Critical Success Factors

A few major issues emerged from the experience of DeVilbiss in implementing its reorganised cell structures. Effective training was critical, and it was important that everyone had the right attitude to the new work practices, especially at senior management level. The approach of implementing the new practices a cell at a time allowed attempts to be made to replicate instances of good practice, and the key to understanding was to "look, see and learn".

The removal of unnecessary hierarchy was needed to allow the business to change from a vertical to a more horizontal process. Understandably, there was resistance to the change by middle managers, who perceived that their roles might no longer be needed. In hard figures, the number of employees was reduced from 374 in 1989 down to 168 at the time of writing, mainly because of the vast increase in the outsourcing of non-strategic components.

DeVilbiss believes that a primary success factor has been the support of its accounts personnel, who are seen as "one of the gang". Their attitudes have changed since they were moved down to the factory floor. Their previous location was described as "living in an ivory tower", detached from the rest of the workers.

DeVilbiss is not only cell-based on the shop floor, but the concept embraces the whole organisation, every function and department. Each element of the business is an autonomous unit and cells may or may not use the skills and services of other cells. The freedom of choice is theirs. For instance certain areas of the business are described as the "yellow pages" units. They can include cells such as general purchasing, lighting maintenance, etc. These are essentially service providers to be used as and when necessary, and can obtain efficiencies and effectiveness working as autonomous units.

# Results

Before reorganisation there was a management structure containing six levels, and it was felt that this was unduly complex. Flattening the hierarchy has reduced this to four, with decisions typically being made at the lowest level possible, and senior managers acting as facilitators rather than controllers. The morale and motivation of shop-floor staff have been greatly improved, a result of their being treated as people with intellectual contributions to make, rather than as mere providers of skilled energy.

There has been a substantial reduction in purchasing and manufacturing complexity, with corresponding reductions in control requirements. Cycle time has been reduced considerably, as have inventory levels. Throughput has increased and DeVilbiss are realising their on-time delivery objectives. Four years ago delivery was a serious problem, with up to 1.7 million overdue components per month. Today they have the figure down to about 4000 per month. Their next objective is to improve production forecasting, as this accounts for three quarters of schedule revisions.

As a direct result of the reorganisation of the DeVilbiss operations into a focused, cell-based environment, cost reductions were realised in virtually all direct costs (see Table A5.1).

*Table A5.1    Cost reductions at DeVilbiss*

| Cost component | % Change | Reasons |
| --- | --- | --- |
| Purchased out | +25% | Due to greater value of bought-out components. |
| Direct labour | −28% | Due to reduced level of internal manufacture. |
| Raw materials | −40% | As above. |
| Tool service | −40% | As above. |
| Holiday pay | −26% | Due to reduced numbers of direct labour. |
| Wages | −36% | Reduction in inspection supervision, etc. |
| Staff overtime | −43% | As above. |
| Stocktaking | −66% | Due to greater visibility provided by cell layout. |
| Scrap | −62% | Due to greater visibility of quality issues. |

# References and Further Reading

Adler P. Time and motion regained. Harvard Business Review, Jan/Feb 1993, pp. 97–108

Adler P and Cole RE. Designed for learning: a tale of two auto plants. Sloan Management Review, Spring 1993, pp. 85–94

Alexander G. Times, 3 May 1992

Antal AB and Merkens H. Cultures and fictions in transition. Journal of General Management, 19(1), 1993

Ayres RU. CIM: A challenge to technology management. International Journal of Technology Management, 7(1–3)

Ayres RU. CIM: Hypothesis. IIASA Conference, IISA, Laxenburg, Austria, 1990

Badham R. Social dimension of CIM. International Labour Review, 130, 1991, pp. 373–392

Badham R. Human centred CIM. Futures, 23(10), 1991, pp. 1050 et seq.

Banham J. The anatomy of change. Butterfield, London, 1994

Barnett C. The audit of war. Macmillan, London, 1986

Belbin J. Management teams. Heinemann, London, 1981

Berggren C. NUMMI vs. Uddevalla. Sloane Management Review, winter 1994, pp. 37–49

Bjerknes G and Ehn P. Computers and democracy – a Scandinavian challenge. Swedish Institute for Work Life Research, Stockholm, 1987

Boje D and Winsor R. The resurrection of Taylorism: total quality management's hidden agenda. Journal of Organisational Change Management, 6(4), 1992, pp. 57–70

Borrie G. Social justice. The report of the commission on social justice. Vintage, London, 1994

Bowen DE and Lawler EE. Sloan Management Review, spring, 1992, pp. 31–39

British Standards Institution. Quality Vocabulary: BS 4788: Part 2, 1991

Brockman J. Information management and total quality. Journal of Information Science Principles and Practice, 19(4), 1993, pp. 259–265

Brodner P. FAST monitor programme. European Commission, Brussels, Feb., 1990

Brodner P. The shape of future technology: the anthropocentric alternative. Springer-Verlag, London, 1990

Burrows P. GE rethinks factory of the future. Electronic Business, 17, 1991, pp. 50–53

Callender C. Will NVQs work? Training Tomorrow, Nov., 1992, pp. 20–22

Camp R. Benchmarking. DTI and HMSO, London, 1989

Champy J. In Hammer M and Champy J. Reengineering the corporation. Harper Collins, New York, 1993

Chew M. Japan's profitable prize. Incentive, 163(9), 1989, pp. 82–86

Ciulla JB. In Freeman R (ed.) Business ethics: the state of the art, Heinemann, London, 1994

Cooley M. Architect or bee: the human price of technology. Hogarth Press, London, 1st edn, 1977

Cooley M. Architect or bee: the human price of technology. Hogarth Press, London, 2nd edn, 1987

Cooley M. European competitiveness in the twenty-first century. EEC FAST, Brussels, 1989

Corbett JM, Rasmussen LB, Rauner F. Crossing the border: the social and engineering design of computer integrated manufacturing systems. Springer-Verlag, London, 1991

Deming WE. Out of the crisis. CUP, 1986

Dickson WJ and Roethlisberger FJ. Management and the worker. Harvard University Press, Cambridge, Mass, 1939.

Drucker P. Post-capitalist society. Butterworth-Heinemann, Oxford, 1993

Drucker P. Post-capitalist society. Financial Times 11 June 1993.

Economist, 5 June 1993, p. 87

Economist Intelligence Unit. On course for success. EIU, London, 1992

Engelbart D. Authorship provisions in augment. Proc Comp Conf, IEEE New York, pp 465–472, 1984

Ennals R. Artificial Intelligence and human institutions. Springer-Verlag, London, 1991

Ennals R. Executive guide to preventing IT disasters, Springer-Verlag, London, 1995

Ennals R and Molyneux P (eds). Managing with information technology. Springer-Verlag, London, 1993

European Commission. The future of industry in Europe. FAST, Brussels, 1993, p. 155

Financial Times 6 March 1992

Financial Times 10 December 1992

Financial Times 5 May 1993

Financial Times 20 May 1993

Financial Times 24 May 1993

Financial Times 26 May 1993

Financial Times 25 June 1993

Financial Times 14 July 1993

Financial Times 8 September 1993

Financial Times 17 September 1993

Financial Times 21 September 1993

Furrer J. Ciba Geigy: consultancy report. Ciba-Geigy, Geneva, 1992

Gill K. Human centred systems: foundational concepts and traditions. In: Ennals R and Molyneux P (eds). Managing with information technology. Springer-Verlag, London, 1993

Göranzon B. The practical intellect. UNESCO/Springer-Verlag, London, 1992

Göranzon B (ed). Skill, technology and enlightenment: on practical philosophy. Springer-Verlag, London, 1995

Göranzon B and Florin M (eds). Artificial intelligence, culture and language: on education and work. Springer-Verlag, London, 1990

Göranzon B and Florin M (eds). Dialogue and technology: art and knowledge, Springer-

Verlag, London, 1991

Göranzon B and Florin M (eds). Skill and education: reflection and experience, Springer-Verlag, London, 1992

Göranzon B and Josefson I (eds). Knowledge, skill and artificial intelligence, Springer-Verlag, London, 1988

Gottschalch J. Research report, UMIST, 1992

Grint K. Research report. Templeton College, Oxford, 1993

Guardian 15 April 1991

Guardian 28 September 1993

Guardian 3 December 1993

Gustavsen B. Dialogue and development. Swedish Institute for Work Life Research, Stockholm, 1992

Hamel G and Prahalad CK. Strategic intent. Harvard Business Review, May–June, 1992

Hammer M and Champy R. Reengineering the corporation. Harper & Row, New York, 1988

Hampden-Turner C and Trompenaars F. The seven cultures of capitalism. Piatkus, London, 1994

Handy C. The age of unreason. Century-Hutchinson, London, 1989

Handy C. The empty raincoat. Hutchinson, London, 1994

Handy C. In Management Today, April, 1989, pp. 82–89

Handy C. Managers in five countries. NEDO, London, 1987

Handy C. Understanding organisations. Penguin, London, 1984

Harvard Business Review, June, 1993, p. 118

Harvard Business Review, December, 1993

Henley Centre for Forecasting. Financial Times, 21 September 1993

Higgs M and Rowland D. All pigs are equal. Management education and development, 23(4), 1992, pp. 349–362

HMSO. Working together: education and training. HMSO, London, 1986

HMSO. New training initiative: a programme for action. HMSO, London, 1987

Human Centred Systems Ltd. BESTMAN project report. HCL, Hemel Hempstead, 1993

Hutton W. The state we're in. Cape, London, 1995

Imai M. Kaizen: the key to Japan's competitive success. 1986

Industrial Relations Review and Report. NVQs – a survey of progress. Issue 534, IRRR, April, 1993, pp. 2-15.

Ingersoll Engineers. The FMS report. IFS, Bradford, 1982

Institute for Management Development/World Economic Forum. World Competitiveness Report. IMD/WEF, Lausanne, Geneva, 1992

Institute of Economic Affairs. Training too much? IEA, London, 1992

Ishikawa K. The Deming Prize. Japanese Union of Scientists and Engineers, Tokyo, 1985

Johansson A. The labour movement and the emergence of Taylorism. Economic and Industrial Democracy, 7, 1986, pp. 449–485

Johansson H et al. Coopers and Lybrand, London, 1993

Kahn J. When bad management becomes criminal. INC, March, 1987, p. 48

Kanter RM. When giants learn to dance. Allen & Unwin, London, 1989

Kay J. The foundations of corporate success. OUP, 1993

Keegan W. The spectre of capitalism. Vintage, London, 1993

Kidd P. Agile Manufacturing. Addison-Wesley, London, 1994

Kidd P. Organisation, people and technology in European manufacturing. FOP 27, vol. 3, Commission of the EU, November, 1990

Knouse S and Carson P. Deming and Taylor: a comparison of two leaders who shaped the world's view of management. International Journal of Public Administration, 16(10m), 1992, p. 1641

Kozik S. Reengineering the company. Cigna, New York, 1992

Kraus K. In Göranzon B and Florin M (eds). Artificial intelligence, culture and language: on education and work. Springer-Verlag, London, 1990

Lilley S. Men, machines and history. Lawrence and Wishart, London, 1965

Mainichi Daily News (Tokyo). No real sense of affluence. 17 January 1989

Marx K. Das Kapital. Berlin, 1872

Marx K. Economic and philosophical manuscripts of 1884

Maskery A. Japanese auto union demands a better life. Automotive News, 17 February 1992, p. 82

Maslow A. Motivation and personality. Harper & Row, New York, 1954

Matsushita K. Not for bread alone. PHP Institute, Tokyo, 1984

Mayo E. The human problems of an industrial civilization. Macmillan, New York, 1933

McGregor D. The human side of enterprise. McGraw-Hill, New York, 1960

MIT. IMPV World Assembly Plant Survey. MIT Press, Cambridge, Mass, 1989

MIT. Management in the 1990s. MIT Press, Cambridge, Mass, 1989

Monod J, Gylenhammar P and Dekker W. Reshaping Europe: a report from the European round table of industrialists, Brussels, 1991

NEDO (National Economic Development Office). Diversifying from defence. HMSO, London, 1991

New C. Research report, Cranfield School of Management, Bedford, 1992

Norman A. Computer insecurity. Chapman & Hall, London, 1983

Oakland J. Total quality management. DTI and HMSO, London, 1989

Ormerod P. The death of economics. Faber, London, 1994

OTR Group. BPR – real or hype? OTR, Brussels, 1993

PA Consulting. Manufacturing into the late 1990s. HMSO, London, 1989

Paine LS. Managing for organisational integrity. Harvard Business Review, March/April 1994, pp. 106–117

Pascale R and Athos AG. The art of Japanese management. Simon & Schuster, New York, 1992

Peer Y. Letter to R. Kaura, 16 February 1994

Person H. The genius of Frederick W. Taylor. Advanced Management, 10 January 1945, pp. 2–11

Peters T and Waterman RH. In search of excellence. Harper & Row, New York, 1982

Peters T. Liberation management. Harper & Row, New York, 1994

Porter M. Competitive advantage. Free Press, New York, 1985

Porter M. The competitive advantage of nations. Free Press, New York, 1990

Polanyi M. The tacit dimension. Routledge & Kegan Paul, London, 1966

Rehder R. Building cars as if people mattered. Columbia Journal of World Business, summer, 1992, p. 58

Reich R. The real economy. Atlantic Monthly, February, 1991.

Reich R. The work of nations. Knopf, New York, 1991

Research Technology Management, 36(1), pp. 49–51

Rose M. Industrial behaviour. Penguin, Harmondsworth, 1988, p. 111

Rosenbrock H. Engineering as an art. Artificial Intelligence and Society, 2(4), October–December, 1988

Rosenbrock H. Machines with a purpose. OUP, Oxford, 1990

Rosenbrock H. (ed). Designing human centred technology: a cross-disciplinary project in computer aided manufacturing. Springer-Verlag, London, 1989

Rosenbrock H. Science, technology and purpose. Artificial Intelligence and Society, 6(1), January–March, 1992

Sandberg A. New Technology, Work and Employment, 8(2), pp. 83–90

Semler R. Maverick! Century, London, 1993

Senge P. The fifth discipline. Doubleday, New York, 1990

Shingo S. Modern approaches to manufacturing improvement: the Shingo system. Productivity Press, Tokyo, 1989

Skinner BF. Science and human behaviour. Random House, New York, 1953

Smedley, I. Financial Times, 17 Sept 1993

Smith A. A theory of moral sentiments [1759]. Bohn, London, 1861

Smith A. The wealth of nations [1776]. Methuen, London, 1904

Smith R and Smith D. Corporate strategy, culture and conversion. Business Strategy Review, summer, 1992, pp. 45–58

Smith T. Accounting for growth. Century, London, 1993

Solomon R. Ethics and excellence: cooperation and integrity in business. 1992

Soros G. The alchemy of finance. Wiley, Chichester, 1994

Taylor FW. Shop management. Norton, New York, 1903

Taylor FW. The principles of scientific management. Norton, New York, 1911

Tempte, T. The chair of Tutankhamun. In Göranzon B and Florin M (eds), Dialogue and technology: art and knowledge. Springer-Verlag, London, 1991

Tempte, T. The practical intellect and master-apprenticeship. In Göranzon B (ed), Skill, technology and enlightenment: on practical philosophy. Springer-Verlag, London, 1995

Thomas M. The Luddites: machine breaking in regency England, 1972

The Times 20 February 1993

The Times 19 August 1993

The Times 30 August 1993

Tubbs W. Karoushi: stress death and the meaning of work. Journal of Business Ethics, 12, 1993, pp. 867–877

Vogel D. The globalisation of business ethics: why America remains distinctive. California Management Review, fall, 1992, pp. 30–49

Voss CA. Success and failure in advanced manufacturing technology. International Journal of Technology Management, 3, 1993, p. 185

Weizenbaum J. Computing power and human reason. Freeman, New York, 1972

Weizenbaum J. Facing reality: computer scientists aid war efforts. Technology Review, 90(1), 1987, pp. 22-23

Wiener N. The human use of human beings. 1950

Winograd T and Flores F. Understanding computers and cognition. Ablex, New York, 1988

Womack J. et al. The machine that changed the world. Rawson, New York, 1990

Wrege C and Greenwood G. Frederick W. Taylor: The father of scientific management: myth and reality. 1991

Zuboff S. In the age of the smart machine. Harvard University Press, Cambridge, Mass, 1988

# Name Index

# Subject Index